MURDER IN VICTORIAN WESTERN MICHIGAN

Michael Delaware

Published by The History Press
An imprint of Arcadia Publishing
Charleston, SC
www.historypress.com

First published 2025

Manufactured in the United States

ISBN 9781467170215

Library of Congress Control Number: 2025935714

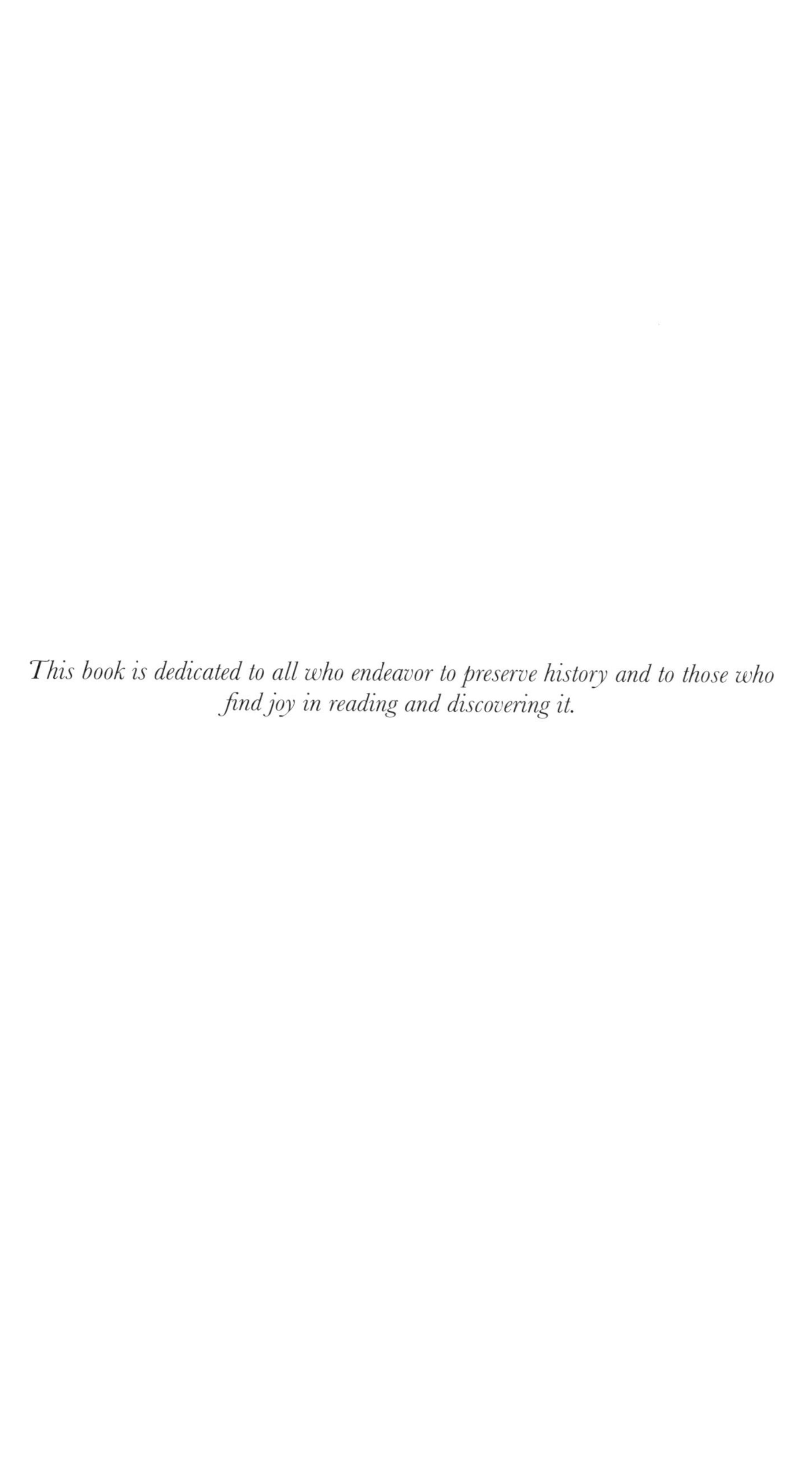

This book is dedicated to all who endeavor to preserve history and to those who find joy in reading and discovering it.

CONTENTS

ACKNOWLEDGEMENTS

As a researcher and author, there are many to whom I owe a debt of gratitude. One truly never takes such a journey alone. It is an impossible task to extend my full appreciation, but I will endeavor to do so.

I will begin by thanking The History Press for once again believing in my work enough to publish my second book. An incredible team of people one and all.

Without a doubt, I owe my greatest thanks to my brother Richard and my sister Jeanne. Both have remained steadfast in their offerings of wise, sensible and sometimes ruthless editing to keep me on track throughout this dark history expedition. Without their tireless reviewing of my work, this book would not have been possible. I love you both.

The following organizations and people all helped me on my journey writing this book, for which I feel truly blessed: The Library of Michigan; Rachel and her team at the Michigan Archives; along with the archives at Willard Library, Kalamazoo Library and University of Michigan; Rhiannon Cizon and the Berrien County Historical Association; Julie Kimmer and the Eaton County Historical Association; the Battle Creek Regional History Museum; the Battle Creek Historical Society; Mollie Watson from the Niles History Center; and the sexton at Silverbrook Cemetery (who kept me from getting lost).

Special thanks to Bobbie Mathis, a genuine friend and fellow historian who was the first to review and edit "A Mysterious Dream and a Missing Boy," encouraging me to include it in this collection. Also, James N. Jackson and Dave Eddy always offer words of encouragement and support when I need it most. There are no words to express my gratitude for your friendship.

Finally, to the amazing librarians, historical societies and other organizations who invited me to present my first book to their members, endless thanks. I also salute my readers, podcast listeners and YouTube followers. You truly are gems, and may you forever sparkle.

INTRODUCTION

This is a new collection of stories following my initial book, *Victorian Southwest Michigan True Crime*.

The Victorian era is explicitly the reign of English Queen Victoria from 1836 until her death in 1901. As a researcher, it was an age that fascinated me most when I began to explore early Michigan history. An astonishing evolution of Western civilization, concurrently in America and Europe, took place during this era. Many milestones of progress, from telecommunications to the railroad, all emerged from this innovative and culturally inspirational time.

Agriculture transitioned from individual farms tilled by oxen and plow to vast fields cultivated by the steam tractor, separator and combine. Long-distance correspondence at the beginning of the era consisted of mail delivered by horseback, later by stagecoach and finally by rail. The telegraph led to telephone exchanges, a precursor to our modern systems. Technological advances in clothing with mass production of sewing machines in the 1850s launched a fashion industry. These are just a few examples, but I was most interested in the people and society as a whole.

Heinous, bloody crimes were uncommon and quite unexpected. When they happened, the ensuing shock to a community was palpable. Angry mobs occasionally swarmed, often threatening to intercede with law enforcement, fervid for justice and eager to punish the accused. You will find examples of this within.

Queen Victoria coronation portrait. *By George Hayter, Royal Collection RCIN 401213.*

Likewise, crime scene examination was not as comprehensive as we find today. Forensic science was almost nonexistent. Police investigations relied heavily on witness testimony, limited medical autopsies and chemical testing performed by professors at the University of Michigan. Labs could provide answers on types of poisons and whether a blood sample was human blood, but beyond this, knowledge was limited.

Criminal charges were often supported solely by circumstantial evidence. Sometimes convictions could be driven by the emotional pulse of the community rather than facts presented at trial. In other cases, eyewitness testimony without any other supporting evidence was enough to convict someone. Notwithstanding, the inevitable quest for justice was sometimes overcast by injustice.

Early prisons were based on the 1790 Walnut Street Prison in Philadelphia, a prototype espousing Quaker optimism that penitence and isolated self-examination would bring salvation, hence the name *penitentiary*.

In 1846, Michigan banned the death penalty. Consequently, convictions for first-degree murder mandated a life sentence of solitary confinement with hard labor.

Brutality plagued the legal system when implementing justice. The solitary confinement cells were windowless brick-walled rooms with low ceilings that inhibited standing. Inmates were forbidden from speaking, given a straw mattress and a wooden pail for human waste and ate their meals in darkness. The smallest infraction often incurred vicious corporal punishment, including whippings, starvation and torture. Measles, tuberculosis, yellow fever and dysentery were prevalent and often fatal. There was no heat, plumbing, electricity or ventilation. Many prisoners went insane or died in these conditions, and humanitarian reform would not come until much later. Accordingly, many convicts died within their first few years of incarceration.

These stories were constructed from newspaper accounts; census, cemetery, property and even prison records; parole board transcripts; contemporary biographical profiles, maps and books, all painstakingly woven together. In writing this book, I spent many hours studying details, cross-referencing varying accounts to adhere to facts. These pages contain not only true crimes but also a few intriguing mysteries.

The Victorian era began in Michigan while the southwestern counties were being settled. At that time, the untamed wilderness was a vast unknown west of Ann Arbor. After days of travel along a rough territorial road, one arrived at the first collection of cabins known as Jacksonopolis (later Jacksonburgh and eventually Jackson). Continuing the journey west, Marshall, Battle Creek and Kalamazoo would emerge from the wilds.

Therefore, in this collection, the events all took place west of Ann Arbor, as far south as Niles and as far north as Manistee and Boyne Falls.

True crime stories are not analogous to fairy tales. A real person without fail meets an undesirable, foreshortened departure from life and happy endings are invariably absent. The only ray of sunshine, if one exists in these dark chronicles, is that they all happened a long time ago. Further, those who committed these crimes have long since become dust.

A fellow historian once told me we all die two deaths. The first death is when our life ends, and the second transpires the last time someone utters our names aloud. With that in mind, let us honor the names of the innocent victims, as well as the heroes, by vocalizing theirs and perhaps maintain a vigilant silence toward the villains—lest they leap from these pages and return to haunt us.

Michael Delaware, 2025

1

BETRAYAL AT THE LEONIDAS CROSSROADS

(1853)

He became engaged to marry Miss Mary Wood, living near Leonidas, in Southwestern Michigan. In 1853, he sold his Vermont farm for several thousand dollars, concealed the money about his person, and started for the home of his fiancée, intending to be married....Mr. Estabrook was never seen again.
—Boston Daily Globe, *March 15, 1883*

Thomas Brown Estabrook was born on March 14, 1812, in Reading, Vermont, to parents Thomas Estabrook and Sybil Brown. His father was a farmer in Windsor Township, and he grew up learning the toils and challenges of that life. His mother was a lineal descendant of Nicholas Brown, the founder of Brown University.

In 1853, at age forty-one, Thomas B. Estabrook sold his own farm in Vermont and traveled to Michigan, where he was to meet his fiancée, Mary Wood, who resided in Mendon Township. She was a single woman, originally from Vermont, who owned eighty acres of land just west of Leonidas in St. Joseph County. Thomas carried the money from the sale of his land on his person when he traveled, as he intended to settle in St. Joseph County after their wedding.

He took the Michigan Southern & Northern Indiana Railroad to Michigan, getting off at the Burr Oak train station, on Saturday, November 12, 1853. Once there, he hired a man named Julius Thompson to take him to a hotel that was not far from the station, where he rented a room and

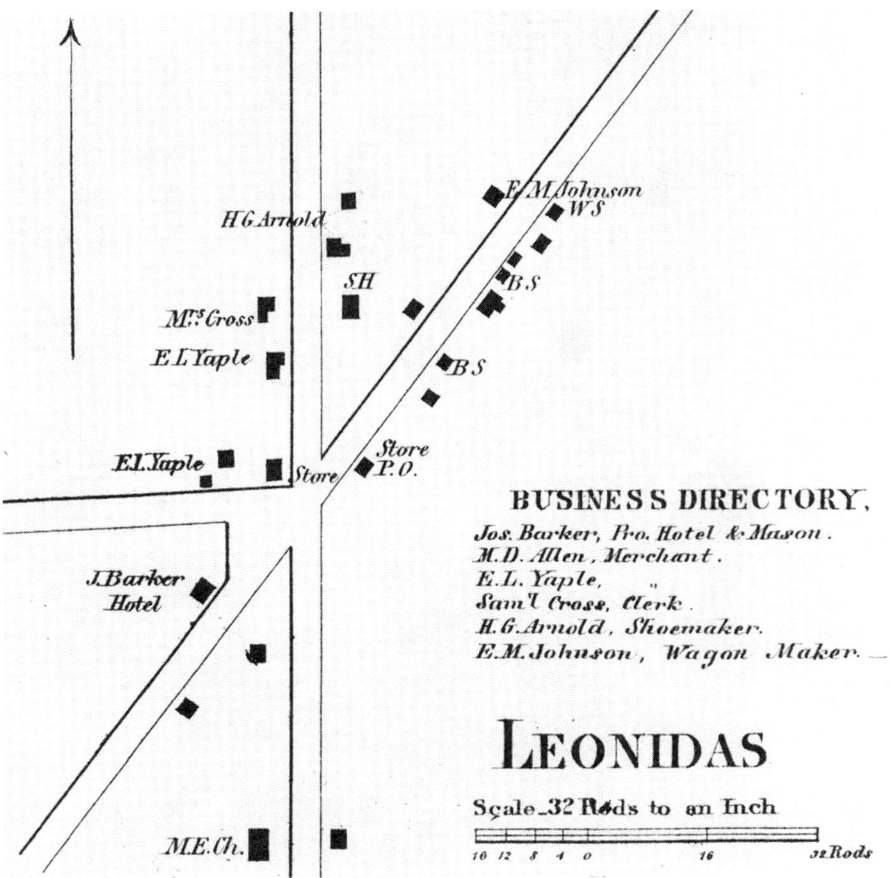

Leonidas in the 1858 Atlas. *Library of Congress.*

deposited his trunks. The next morning, on Sunday, he hired Thompson again to take him and the larger of his two trunks with his wagon and team to the farm of Miss Wood.

On the way, they stopped at noon for a meal in the tavern at the crossroads in Leonidas. The community was then known as Leonidas Corners and was about three or four miles east from the end of his journey. All the while, the weather conditions were worsening, with a wintry mix etching deep, muddy ruts into the road, bogging down the wheels of the wagon.

Because the conditions of the weather were becoming more and more treacherous, Thompson would take Thomas no further. Although eager to return, Thompson remained for a time and had dinner with Thomas. After their meal together, Thompson departed for Burr Oak.

The tavern was kept by Haywood and Stillwell, and there Thomas hired a man to travel to Burr Oak the next day to pick up his smaller trunk and deliver it to the Wood farm.

Thomas inquired at the tavern to see if there was anyone who could take him and his large trunk the final three miles that day, and there was no one. Undaunted, he decided to store his trunk at the hotel, planning to make arrangements the next day to pick it up. He proceeded to undertake the final three miles of his journey on foot. When he left the tavern in the twilight of an early wintry evening headed west, this was the last anyone saw of Thomas alive.

Missing

The nuptial ceremony with his betrothed was to be held on her farm the following day. On that day, his large trunk was delivered to the residence; the man who delivered it, unbeknownst to the family at the time, was hired by Haywood, the Leonidas tavernkeeper. The deliveryman relayed a message that Thomas would be along shortly and left.

Much to the disappointment of friends and family on the day of the ceremony, Thomas did not arrive. Nor did he arrive the following day. No one seemed to know where he was, nor had anyone heard from him. His trunk was opened, and it contained his garments, including his wedding clothes, as well as some money and other personal items, but no other clues.

Inquiries were made at the tavern in Leonidas, yet no one had seen him after he left the evening two days earlier. Concerned letters were written to his family in Vermont about his disappearance as the late autumn weather gradually yielded to the increasingly bitter intensity of winter.

After word reached the family in Vermont, Thomas's brother Adin Estabrook made plans to travel to Michigan as soon as weather permitted. He was determined to retrace his brother's steps and uncover what happened to him. The following February, in 1854, Adin arrived at the same Burr Oak train station and also hired Julius Thompson to take him to the tavern in Leonidas. Thompson described his experiences with Adin's brother to him, along with all of the circumstances that took place on the way. Adin learned that Thomas had left money with the landlord of the tavern to arrange for forwarding his trunks to Wood's farm.

After retracing Thomas's steps all the way to the tavern, Adin began to suspect foul play. He made contact with St. Joseph County Sheriff John Hull and others about his brother's disappearance. The witnesses who last saw him were interrogated by Sheriff Hull about their interaction with Thomas, in an effort to determine his whereabouts. Later in the spring, the sheriff finally got a break in the case.

Confession

On May 23, 1854, twenty-seven-year-old Giles Harding, a frequent miscreant in the area of Leonidas, was arrested on the charge of larceny after he stole some plows from a local farm. While Harding was in the jail in nearby Centreville, the sheriff began to question him about his involvement in the disappearance of Estabrook. Witnesses had informed the sheriff that Harding was seen with the missing man before he disappeared. Under the pressure of interrogation, Harding confessed to being an accomplice in murdering the man. This was the first time the death of Thomas Estabrook had been confirmed.

Harding explained to the sheriff that two men, Samuel Ulum and Amos White, had overheard a few days before Estabrook's arrival that he was coming to Leonidas. They learned he had intentions to purchase property and would be traveling with some money on him. Anticipating he might stop at the tavern, they made plans to waylay and murder him and take the money for themselves. Harding claimed he came upon them on the road between Leonidas Corners and Kidd's Mill and overheard them discussing the plans. The two men then enlisted him in the plot under threat of death if he did not participate.

He reported that Thomas, after leaving the tavern on the Sunday evening of November 13, had begun walking west along the road in the direction of Mendon, toward the Wood farm. He had gotten as far as the junction of a new road near the land owned by David Kidd, which had recently been cut in for the purpose of hauling lumber.

There, as if by accident, Thomas Estabrook encountered Amos White and Samuel Ulum sitting with a team of horses and a wagon. Harding said White and Ulum had inquired which way Thomas was heading, and when he told them, they informed him they were also headed in the direction of Wood's farm. They offered Thomas a ride, and he agreed and got in with them. A few moments later, the wagon passed Giles Harding walking along the same road, and he also hopped in.

Harding explained that the four men headed down the road together, with White driving and Estabrook sitting beside him. Harding and Ulum were in the back. Distracting Estabrook with conversation, White had steered the wagon north, instead of west, along the logging road. When they had gone about thirty rods (approximately 165 yards), Ulum took a club out from under his coat and struck Thomas on the head from behind. Thomas reportedly cried out, "Oh, dear, I am dead!"

Following that outburst, White took out a knife and stabbed Thomas in the heart. Then all three stripped him of his clothes and money and divided their loot among themselves. White and Ulum dragged Estabrook's body off into the woods and buried the body under an old root or stump. Harding claimed to not see exactly where they buried him, as he remained behind with the horses and wagon.

Harding said that they had gotten about $800 from the dead man's pockets and that he had personally taken Estabrook's boots. Harding then showed the sheriff that he was wearing the same boots.

The other two men had struck and stabbed Thomas, Harding asserted, and all he had done was hold the horses and take the boots along with his portion of the money. He also said that the other two men threatened to kill him if he told anyone.

Harding was in jail when he made this confession. Arrested for larceny, Harding had the reputation of being a notorious liar, whereas White and Ulum had no record.

Without examining this disparity, the sheriff, following Harding's confession, arrested Amos White and Samuel Ulum and charged all three men with first-degree murder. White and Ulum stated they had no knowledge of the crime and maintained their innocence.

All three men were housed in the old log jail in Centreville. The condition of the jail that summer was stifling and made worse when, due to illness, the presiding Judge Whipple was unable to hold the June term in the court. The men sat in that jail all summer long in a space no larger than a common shed, awaiting the recovery of the magistrate.

Search for a Body

Meanwhile, the sheriff organized a search for the body of Thomas Estabrook. The searchers combed the area of woods described by Harding with no success. By the time the case went to trial, the remains had still not been found. White and Ulum, despite efforts by the sheriff to extract a confession, still denied any knowledge of the murder or events that Harding described.

Despite Harding's reputation and the fact that there was no recovered body of the victim, the trial proceeded. The prosecution's case was based entirely on the confession and accusations made by Harding.

Harding included other details of events that supposedly happened in the months following the murder. He claimed Ulum had threatened him on many occasions to keep quiet or he would kill him. He also stated at trial that he asked Ulum on a few occasions where the body was located and was only told that "it was taken care of, and would never be found on dry land."

Centreville Courthouse, 1858. From the 1858 Atlas of St. Joseph County. *Library of Congress.*

White and Ulum maintained their innocence. Harding, hoping for a reduced sentence, cooperated with the prosecution. White had his trial in Centreville, and Ulum was tried in Kalamazoo. They were both defended by John Van Arman from Marshall, the best-known criminal lawyer in the state of Michigan.

Rebuttal witnesses for the prosecution were presented and testified to seeing all three men in the vicinity of Leonidas on the afternoon and evening before the murder was alleged to have occurred. Harding even took Adin Estabrook to the location where he said the body was left in the woods, and there appeared to be a visible impression in the frozen ground where it may have been laid.

Harding maintained that Ulum and White had moved the body the next day but would not tell him where. Suspicions fell on the hotel owners, Hayward and Stillwell, and rumors circulated that they had buried the body in the cellar. An investigation was done in the cellar, digging into every inch of the floor. They also tore down the walls, probed the foundation, ripped up planks in the stables, reopened an old well on the property and dragged every brook, pool or pond on or near the premises, all to no avail.

Convictions

White was found guilty of murder in the first degree at his trial in Centreville, despite a good defense, on October 10, 1854. The trial for Ulum in Kalamazoo lasted fifteen days. The jury went into deliberations on March 26, 1855, and, after only being gone fifteen minutes, returned with a verdict of guilty of murder in the first degree.

Adin Estabrook described White and Ulum after their trials in a letter to the *Vermont Standard* newspaper:

> *Their history is a very dark one. They are over fifty years of age, have large families, and lived by crime and plunder until trapped as murderers in Leonidas, Michigan. They followed their business first in New York, next in Pennsylvania, then in Indiana, and lastly where they were tried and condemned. Their career and end speak in thunder tones the warning which every man commencing in life should heed.*

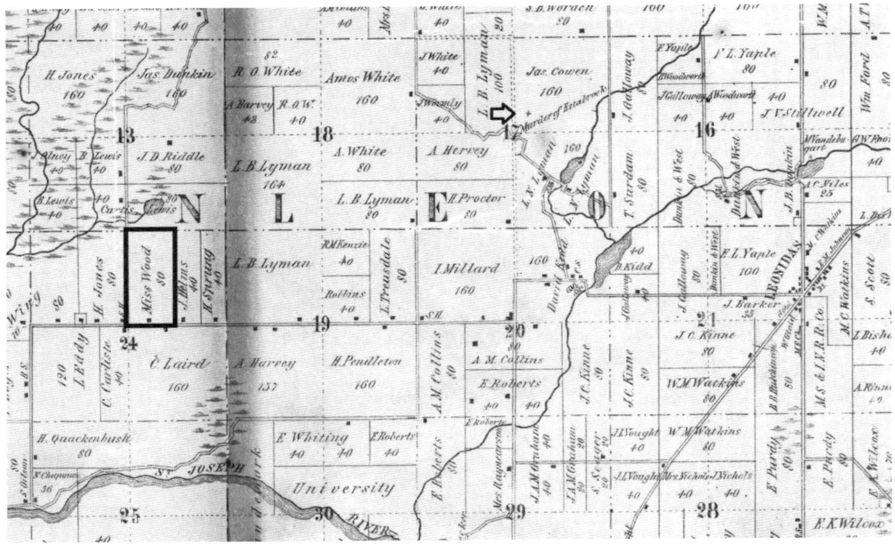

An 1858 Atlas showing the murder site, Wood Farm and Leonidas. *Library of Congress.*

Giles Harding was tried in Centreville for aiding and abetting in the murder. He was found guilty on September 13, 1855. All three men were sentenced to life in prison in solitary confinement at the Michigan State Penitentiary in Jackson.

Thomas Estabrook's body was eventually found on May 13, 1858, around the time of the survey of the county for the 1858 Atlas. The location of his body was considered to be so significant at the time that the surveyor marked on this map an *X* where Estabrook was found, on a lot once owned by Ulum. After the discovery, over one hundred people went over to the property to see the remains.

The skeleton lay just north along the logging road described by Giles Harding on a 160-acre parcel owned by Jason Cowen. A man was walking in the woods and noticed a depression in the earth that resembled a grave. Curious, he took a shovel and dug down, discovering the skeleton. The skull was examined, revealing a heavy fracture just above the ear from a blunt weapon, consistent with the testimony of Giles Harding. Approximately two weeks before the find, Amos White died in prison on Sunday, April 25. He maintained his innocence to his death.

Giles Harding died in prison on April 19, 1875. Before his death, he wrote an affidavit declaring his whole testimony against White and Ulum to be false, divulging he committed the crime himself. He confessed to burying the body on land formerly owned by Ulum, right where the body had been discovered.

Released

As a result, Samuel Ulum petitioned to be released from prison and eventually received a pardon from Michigan Governor Josiah Begole on March 6, 1883, after almost a quarter century of incarceration.

Newspapers across the country carried the story about a man who was wrongly convicted of murder and served nearly thirty years. However, Adin Estabrook wrote a decisive letter to the *Fitchburg Sentinel* newspaper in Massachusetts that described in detail his search for his brother and the investigation that followed. He maintained that there was credible evidence presented at trial from witnesses who saw the three men together just before Thomas disappeared.

Additionally, he had spent time with Harding during the investigation and believed the man was "too idiotic to tell a lie." He recalled seeing the depression of his brother's body in the ground and seeing clumps of his hair that were left behind, having been frozen to the earth before the body was later moved. This experience, combined with testimony from other witnesses at the trials, convinced him that Harding was telling the truth at the trial and that his deathbed affidavit was a lie.

Early on, Adin suspected the hotel proprietors were involved, believing they deliberately detained Thomas from noon until four o'clock in the afternoon, when he finally left on foot and was later murdered. Adin was around those men for eighteen months during the investigation working with the sheriff and considered their recounting of the events on that evening suspicious.

In Burr Oak, Adin located Thomas's smaller trunk, which had never been retrieved. He discovered that Hayward, and not Thomas, had been the one who paid to have the larger trunk sent to the farm the next day. This was the one opened by Mary Wood. This further solidified his belief that the tavernkeepers were hiding something and may very well have been involved in hiding his brother's body over the winter until it could be eventually buried on Ulum's property following the spring thaw.

POSTSCRIPT

Samuel Ulum passed away the year following his release on November 27, 1884, in Mendon, Michigan.

Originally a teacher in Vermont, Adin Estabrook remained in Michigan for two years, where he served as the principal at the academy in Centreville until the murderers of his brother were sentenced to life in prison. In 1856, he returned to Reading, Vermont, where he married Emma Tarbell of Granville, Vermont, on January 15, 1857.

The couple later moved to Lunenburg, Massachusetts. Adin held the position as postmaster from 1860 through 1864 and served as a recruiting officer during the Civil War. He ran for the Massachusetts state legislature in 1875 and was elected to serve as the representative for the Fifth Worcester District of Lunenburg. He served in the legislature for over two decades.

Throughout his life, Adin was renowned for his storytelling skills, good humor and industry in farming. In January 1917, Adin and Emma celebrated their sixtieth wedding anniversary together with their two daughters. Adin passed away on February 9 at the age of eighty-eight. Emma, ailing in grief, passed away from heart failure one month later.

Headstone of Sheriff John Hull, Peek Cemetery, Constantine, Michigan. *Findagrave.com.*

Sheriff John Hull was only elected to serve two terms (1850 and 1852), and his second term ended about a year after the arrest of Ulum, White and Harding. Hull was better known in his day as a musician, having formed the famous Hull & Arnold Orchestra in 1836. For forty years, the orchestra was reputed to have performed all over southwest Michigan and northern Indiana.

What became of the remains of Thomas Estabrook is unknown. His skeleton was discovered two years after Adin had returned east. He is not found in the family plot in Massachusetts. He may have been interred in the Leonidas Cemetery in an unmarked grave, but there is no record of him in any cemetery in St. Joseph County.

It is unknown whether the Estabrook family was ever notified of the discovery. Sheriff Hull, who had been the one Adin had reported the matter to originally when his brother went missing, kept him informed throughout the investigation but was no longer in office when the body was found.

2
SHOTS IN THE DARK
THE KALAMAZOO JAILBREAK (1867)

Resolved, that we, the members of his regiment, hold it to be a sacred duty, resting upon each and all of us, to use every means in our power to search out and bring to justice the vile murderer of our beloved commander.
—Detroit Free Press, *December 18, 1867*

Benjamin Franklin Orcutt first saw the light of day on February 9, 1815, under the shadow of the Green Mountains in Roxbury, Vermont. He obtained his early education at the Randolph Academy in Orange County, Vermont.

Benjamin Franklin Orcutt, 1861. *From History of Kalamazoo, 1880.*

In 1834, at the age of nineteen, infused with the spirit of adventure offered by the newly open lower counties of southwest Michigan, he made his way up the Erie Canal to Lake Ontario, then down the Niagara River, finally stopping in Detroit for a few months after crossing Lake Erie. Orcutt then moved to Chicago for about a year and subsequently moved again, this time settling in Allegan, Michigan, for approximately the same amount of time, moving one final time in 1836 to Kalamazoo, Michigan.

A Man of Service

In 1841, Orcutt was elected constable and was later a deputy U.S. marshal for a few years. When the conflict that was to become known as the Mexican-American War began in 1846, he enlisted in Captain Frederick W. Curtenius's Company A, First Michigan Volunteers, and served in the capacity of first sergeant.

Captain Frederick W. Curtenius. *U of M Bentley Historical Library—Milton Chase Collection.*

When he returned home to Kalamazoo, he worked as a deputy sheriff in Kalamazoo County. In 1854, he was elected sheriff and held that office for four years.

In October 1856, he married Emily Swadel, the daughter of Samuel Swadel of Galesburg. Together they would have three boys: William, followed by twin sons Benjamin and Frank.

When the American Civil War (then referred to as the "War of the Rebellion") erupted in 1861, Orcutt entered the Twenty-Fifth Michigan Infantry and served as a lieutenant colonel from September 24, 1862, through June 9, 1865. His time during the war was regarded by those who served with him as one of conspicuous gallantry and ability. Following the conflict, he returned to Michigan and was again elected sheriff of Kalamazoo County.

The Old Jail

Orcutt assumed the duties of sheriff several years prior to a new county jail being erected. The old jail was known to be an unsecure building and required constant vigilance to prevent the escape of prisoners. It was a free-standing building next to the house the sheriff lived in with his wife.

The jail and courthouse were located on the corner of Main and Rose Streets, across from a few hotels with boardinghouses to the north and in proximity to four houses of worship—the Dutch Reformed, First Baptist, First Congregational and St. Luke's Episcopal Churches—to the west. To the south lay Bronson Park and to the east a block containing multiple businesses, the firehouse and the First Presbyterian Church.

On nights with no deputies on duty, Sheriff Orcutt would be on high alert for any sounds coming from the direction of the jail. Throughout his tenure, several prisoners indicated during their confinement that they would attempt escape, so Orcutt was constantly on the lookout for indications of noise that such an attempt was underway. As a result, this occupied his mind constantly. He became a very light sleeper while on duty.

Disturbance in the Night

On the morning of December 3, 1867, Sheriff Orcutt was aroused from his sleep around three o'clock by an unusual noise he could not identify. Hastily rising from his bed, he dressed quickly, seized his revolver and stepped out into the night. Looking in the direction of the jail, he saw the silhouettes of two men lurking in the shadows. Supposing them to be escaped prisoners, he cocked his revolver and ordered them to halt. They did not obey his commands.

Instead, startled by the order in the dark, the two men ran quickly to the east across Rose Street, with the sheriff pursuing them. Orcutt paused only to fire a round at them, as they disappeared into an alley near Bartlett's Bookstore, attempting to hide beneath a large burr oak tree.

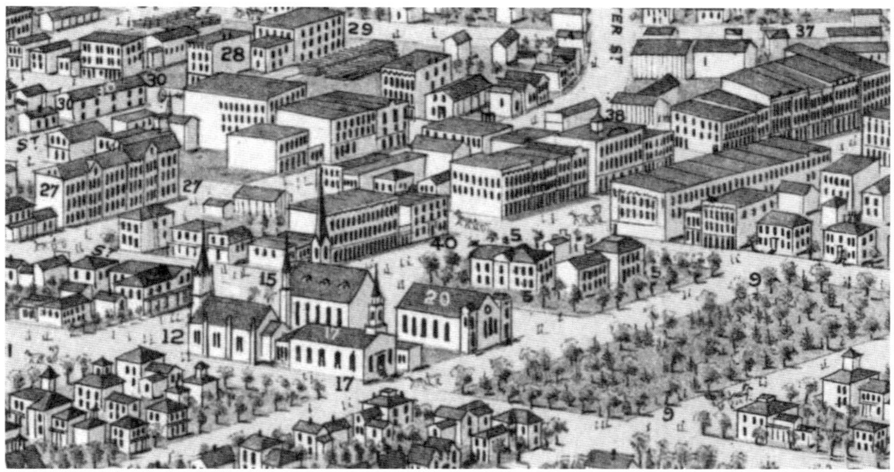

Courthouse and jail indicated as #5 on the Kalamazoo 1874 map. *Library of Congress*.

As the sheriff closed the distance to their location, one of the men fired a gun back at Orcutt three times from the shadows. One of the bullets struck him in the shoulder above the right collarbone. Orcutt staggered backward toward his dwelling and was soon met by his wife near the gate. She noticed he was breathing heavily, but it was dark. Emily supposed he was just winded as a result of the excitement from the chase.

By this time, the alarm had spread throughout the community. People awakened by the sounds of gunshots began to cautiously exit their dwellings and gather on the street.

Two local citizens who had been staying in a rooming house across the street, Daniel Fisher and George W. Taylor, came over to see if they could assist. The sheriff insisted on personally rushing around to the corner of the jail, where he supposed some of the prisoners had escaped.

Wounded

Neither his wife nor any bystander in the darkness was aware that Orcutt had been shot. Only when he became satisfied the assembled crowd would prevent any more prisoners from escaping was he willing to return to his own home.

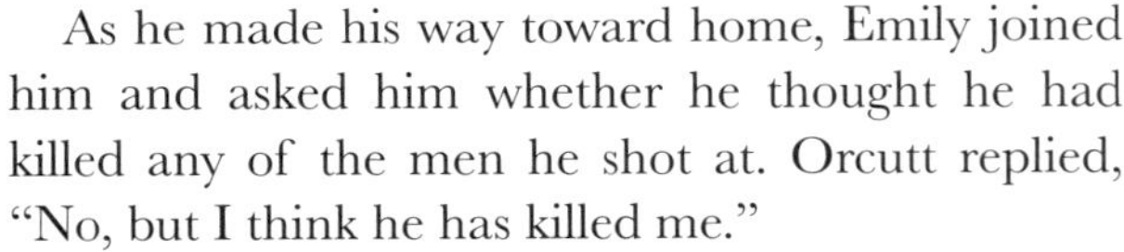

Emily Orcutt, 1863. *Findagrave.com.*

As he made his way toward home, Emily joined him and asked him whether he thought he had killed any of the men he shot at. Orcutt replied, "No, but I think he has killed me."

For the first time, Emily became aware that her husband was wounded. She called for assistance. Neighbors helped guide him into the house, where there was a place to lie down and candlelight to examine him by. Someone sent for a doctor, and soon the wound was examined.

At first, although his condition was quite precarious, there remained a faint hope he might recover. However, the doctor would soon realize the bullet had penetrated his artery, and Orcutt's condition was dire. He was quickly fading into a weakened state.

Morning Light

In the morning light, a jack-screw, tarred rope and kit of burglar's tools was found in the alley where the fleeing men had last been seen by the sheriff. This satisfied investigators that the men who had fired on Orcutt had been an outside party attempting to release prisoners from inside the jail.

Although a number of tools were also found inside the jail, likely passed through a window, it was determined that none of the prisoners had escaped. Thirteen prisoners were still contained within. Three burglars, four bogus detectives charged with arson, two horse thieves and four others on lesser charges.

Orcutt had prevented the would-be rescuers from freeing anyone locked up; however, they did discover one of the three burglars within was now in possession of a revolver that had been passed to him through the bars. He was quickly disarmed and shackled.

The three burglars were James Raymond, O.H. Stone and W.G. Earls from Chicago. They had been caught in Schoolcraft in November trying to break into a safe. The three had been conducting a safe-robbing business between Niles, Schoolcraft and Kalamazoo over a several-week period, stealing over $12,000. They were tracked down by a Detective McFarland from Chicago, and he was assisted in the arrest by Sheriff Orcutt. They landed in the Kalamazoo jail after two of them were caught by Orcutt sleeping on a train during the day, while the third had been watching the place they intended to rob that night.

It was also revealed that the sheriff's shots at the duo that morning outside the jail had wounded at least one of them, as blood was found in the location they were last seen.

The excitement that followed the predawn escape attempt and subsequent shooting of the sheriff sparked anger and upset in the community. A large number of citizens boiled over in rage, and by nine o'clock that morning, many were determined to march to the jail and lynch the prisoner who had been found with the gun, as he was clearly involved with the culprits. Finally, however, cooler heads prevailed.

A mass meeting of the citizens was instead assembled at the courthouse, and a former general, Dwight May, presided over the impromptu meeting.

Many of the men in attendance had served with Orcutt when he was a lieutenant colonel, and they in turn spoke at this gathering, turning the direction of the energy toward an organized manhunt rather than something else. A committee of five men was appointed to take every possible measure to locate and arrest the guilty parties.

The men selected were John Baker, Thomas C. Brownell, David Fisher and George Gale, along with retired sheriff Michael O'Brien. Telegrams were sent in all directions alerting law enforcement of the events, and a thorough investigation of the evidence was made to try to locate the criminals.

Conductors of the different trains leading into the area were furnished with what limited descriptions they had of the culprits, and several suspicious-looking persons were identified from the memory of the men who worked there. The search was on.

THE DEATH OF BENJAMIN F. ORCUTT

Sheriff Orcutt lingered in a weakened condition for nine days until Thursday, December 12, when he quietly passed away at nine o'clock in the evening. It had been a week of dashed hopes and prayers from his wife, who remained by his side.

Benjamin Franklin Orcutt, circa 1861. *Findagrave.com.*

The wound having penetrated an artery, even with round-the-clock care, the doctors were not able to repair the damage. Their best efforts were unsuccessful.

His death cast a dark shadow over the whole community. All of the businesses stopped operations to have time for personal bereavement. The courthouse was draped in black cloths for mourning, and General Dwight May held a soldier's meeting where resolutions were passed to honor Orcutt and committees were organized for his funeral.

His funeral was a solemn and imposing event in Kalamazoo, and a vast concourse of people turned out to honor their fallen sheriff and war hero.

Over 250 former soldiers attended, a large number being from the Twenty-Fifth Michigan Infantry Regiment, with which he had served.

In the service, Orcutt was recognized as both a citizen and a soldier. He was interred at Mountain Home Cemetery, and the expenses for the service were defrayed by the county.

Answers Demanded, Suspects Hunted

Suspicions still haunted the community that the three burglars in the jail knew the identities of the two men who had attempted the jailbreak and murdered the sheriff. Even on the day of his funeral, there were those who wanted to march over to the jail and lynch them unless they gave up the names of the culprits.

As the funeral cortege returned from the cemetery, having witnessed Orcutt's heartbroken wife, Emily, at the service, a large crowd of some 1,500 people collected in front of the jail, holding a demonstration, with some crying out, "Bring them out! Hang them!"

Despite this, the jail was guarded by a large, well-armed volunteer force, and this dampened the enthusiasm of those gathered. Eventually, as the day wore on, the crowd disbursed and committed no acts to disparage the name of the city.

On December 20, a confession was finally obtained from one of the prisoners confined to the jail. By what means or methods this confession was extracted has been lost to history. Nonetheless, the prisoner revealed the names of three men who were alleged to have been involved with planning the jailbreak. Their names were Richard Edwards, Gus Shaw and Walter Williams. They had organized their plan in Chicago, intending to break out the three burglars, and he estimated they had fled back to that city when their plans failed.

Edwards and Williams were ultimately arrested in Chicago on a Wednesday, and Williams accompanied the arresting officer back to Kalamazoo. Edwards insisted on their obtaining a requisition for his transfer to Michigan, which delayed his arrival by a few days. Both were determined to not have been in Kalamazoo the night of the attempted jailbreak. However, they revealed they were involved with the burglary ring and knew the names of two men who were responsible for shooting Sheriff Orcutt.

Initially, only one of the names was released to the public, and that was Gus Shaw, who was still at large. A reward of $1,000 was subsequently offered by the citizens of Kalamazoo for the capture of Shaw, and the hunt continued for him. During this time, John Henry Wells was appointed as sheriff of Kalamazoo County.

With the help of a Detective Dickerson in Chicago, the other man was identified as Hugh Darragh. Darragh was a pickpocket, and whenever he felt the law was on his trail, he would disappear and show up in another city. Detective Dickerson helped Sheriff Wells hunt Darragh down after he left Chicago.

In January 1868, Dickerson followed Darragh and arrested him in New York. The thirty-two-year-old, blue-eyed, brown-haired Darragh was easy to identify by a tattoo with the letters *HD* on his right hand and another of a star surrounded by dots on his left arm.

Working with the police there, they held him for transfer to Michigan. Sheriff Wells went to New York and returned with Darragh on January 9, after getting a requisition approved by the governor of Michigan.

Darragh confessed that he was afraid to return to Kalamazoo, for fear of being lynched. It was learned through interrogation that Darragh was not the man who fired on Sheriff Orcutt that early morning when the jailbreak was attempted. However, he firmly identified the shooter as being Gus Shaw.

A few weeks later, around January 15, it was reported that one of the burglars in the Kalamazoo jail had succeeded in making a saw and sawed off his shackles. He and two other prisoners were attempting to light a fire against an exterior wall to burn their way out of the jail. Their plans were detected by the jailers, and all three were thrown into leg irons to prevent any further attempts.

Hugh Darragh was tried and convicted on September 14, 1868, for aiding prisoners to escape and was sentenced to six years at the Michigan State Penitentiary in Jackson. He died in prison on July 17, 1873, fourteen months before completing his term.

ALIAS "GUS SHAW"

The hunt for the man named Gus Shaw continued. It wasn't until January 1869, a year later, that the name Gus Shaw was discovered to be an alias used by a man named Stephen Boyle, who was also known to use another alias, Edward Francis. On February 1, Boyle was finally arrested in New York City while he was attempting to rob a jewelry store.

Boyle was part of a group of thieves known as the Butcher Cart Gang, whose name was derived from their modus operandi of using a light butcher cart to which a fleet horse was attached. Their method consisted mostly of robbing bank messengers or other persons known to have large amounts of money in their possession. If the robbery was successful, they would jump into the cart and it would be driven off by a confederate holding the reins of the horse, running away at breakneck speed before the victim could recover from the surprise.

The operation went on in New York for about a year, and because the perpetrators acted so speedily, the victims often did not get a glimpse of the robbers' features and thus were unable to identify them. Stephen Boyle, however, was a known ruffian in the city, and was one of the three suspects identified as part of the Eleventh Ward Butcher Cart thieves by witnesses.

During their time of operation, the three men had robbed the Farmers and Citizens Bank of Williamsburg of $20,000, gotten away with $16,000 from a large carpet manufacturing messenger and stolen over $1 million in checks from a messenger of the Bank of New York. The checks were returned secretly to the superintendent of the police department as a mock Christmas present by the men in December 1868, as they were considered worthless to the robbers.

Boyle was captured by a police officer who had surveilled him outside of a jewelry store. Suspecting the officer, Boyle fired a revolver at him. He then jumped into the cart, and his partners proceeded to try to ride away. Before Boyle had climbed fully into the cart, the officer, who had been missed by the bullet, grabbed his leg and pulled him from the cart as it rode off. The cart later collided with a railroad car, and the other occupants scattered, escaping from the police. Boyle was arrested and later confessed to several other robberies in New York with the gang.

He also freely confessed to shooting Sheriff Orcutt when questioned about it and admitted he had been on the run for over a year. He too was afraid to be returned to Michigan for fear of the citizens of Kalamazoo lynching him.

Boyle was taken to the police station in New York. Initially, he was held awaiting a requisition from Governor Baldwin of Michigan after being identified as the murderer of Sheriff Orcutt by a Detective Bennett, who indicated Boyle was wanted in Kalamazoo.

While there, a large group of roughs congregated in the vicinity of police headquarters, determined to overpower the police and free Boyle. However, a detective discovered the intentions of those gathering and obtained strong reinforcements, whereupon the crowd was dispersed.

At Boyle's arraignment a few weeks later for the robbery crimes in New York, Sheriff Wells appeared with papers he presented to the district attorney requesting Boyle be released into his custody to return him for trial in Kalamazoo. If Boyle was to be returned, he would have faced life in prison in solitary confinement were he convicted of first-degree murder, as Michigan had done away with the death penalty. This was a much more severe punishment than was potentially facing him in New York.

The judge considered this but was furious when he learned of the attempt to free Boyle. He denied Sheriff Wells his request, wanting to make an example of the class of thieves that had recently descended on New York to infest the city with crime. Rather than release Boyle to Michigan, the judge decided to prosecute him in New York and, if convicted, planned to give him the maximum allowed penalty under the law to teach a lesson to these other thieves.

If Boyle for some reason was not convicted of the robbery charges, the judge indicated he would release him to the custody of the sheriff. The outcome was that Boyle was indeed convicted of the robbery charges in New York, and the judge sentenced him to forty years in the Sing Sing Correctional Facility.

Legacy

In 1872, a prominent monument was erected near the grave of Benjamin Franklin Orcutt at a cost of $600, raised by the citizens of Kalamazoo. It honored his service in the war and bore a shield and an obelisk engraved on three sides with the following inscriptions:

> *Erected by his fellow citizens as a token of regard.*
> *Lieut. Col. B.F. Orcutt. 25th Mich. Vol. Inf'ty War of 1861 Died 1867 AE 53.*
> *In war, a soldier: In peace, the citizen's guardian.*
> [The abbreviation AE on the engraving stands for age (or aged), from the Latin anno aetatis suae, which means "in the specified year of a person's age."]

Orcutt Marker in Mountain Home Cemetery, Kalamazoo. *Author collection.*

The Michigan state legislature further passed an act authorizing the county to levy a tax of $2,000 to be given to his surviving widow as assistance. However, when the vote came before the board of supervisors in Kalamazoo, it was voted down. In the years that followed, many other attempts were made for lesser amounts, but none of the proposals passed. The county never provided any funds for Orcutt's family beyond covering the cost of his funeral.

When the Kalamazoo post of the Grand Army of the Republic (GAR) was organized in the years following his death, the Civil War veterans adopted the name Post Orcutt in his honor.

Emily Orcutt raised her three sons on her own and never remarried. She lived the rest of her days in Kalamazoo passing away at the age of sixty-eight following a case of pneumonia in 1905. Known for organizing the Kalamazoo Women's Relief Corps, she was very prominent in charitable work within the community. Emily Orcutt was the last living pensioner of the Mexican-American War in Kalamazoo at the time of her death.

Their oldest son, William, went on to own and operate a hardware store in Roscommon, Michigan. He died in 1929 and is buried in the Roscommon Village Cemetery. Frank remained with his mother in Kalamazoo, working for the post office until his death at the age of seventy-four in 1933. He is buried in Mountain Home Cemetery alongside his mother and father. His twin brother, Benjamin, became a railroad engineer in Utah and later moved to Montana, where he passed away at the age of seventy-five in 1934. He is buried in Butte, Montana.

Today the Orcutt monument stands vigil atop a small rise in the southwest corner of Mountain Home Cemetery, across the street from the Admission Center at Kalamazoo College.

3

SUNSET ON THE SPIRIT OF THE WOODS

(1869)

The iron doors close, the gloom of the cell, bordering on the gloom of the grave—heaven's sunlight is shut out and dark despair settles around. If guilty, justice has been done; if innocent, God in mercy right the wrong.

—History of Manistee, Mason & Oceana Counties, Michigan, *1882*

The city of Manistee lies on the eastern shore of that great inland sea known as Lake Michigan, some eighty miles north of Muskegon in the very heart of the famous Michigan fruit belt.

The River

The Ojibwa people first attached the name Manistee to the principal river in the region. Some local sources say the word means "river with islands at its mouth," but others claim it translates more precisely to "spirit of the woods."

The first white people to land on those shores were a party of men from Massachusetts who arrived on boats in 1832. They constructed a blockhouse but were confronted by the Ojibwa and compelled to desist.

The next known settlers were the brothers John and Joseph Stronach in 1841, who constructed a water mill on the Little Manistee River. When the

Ojibwa became determined to drive him off, John managed to negotiate a treaty of peace by offering them a barrel of pork and another of flour. More settlers arrived by 1849, and the Ojibwa reservation was dismantled through treaty and the land sold.

For the next twenty years, the small town of Manistee grew to a beautiful little city of 271 inhabitants and sat amid a township of roughly 3,000 total residents by the late 1860s. The city lying mostly along the banks of the Manistee River, stretching two miles from the great lake, was so remote it was virtually invisible and nameless to the rest of Michigan.

However, the tragedy that occurred in this small rural community in September 1869 achieved notoriety that spread across the state for the two years that followed. During the following decades, many people would remember only that Manistee was connected with this crime but know little else about the community.

About three-quarters of a mile from Lake Michigan, near a bridge crossing in the heart of Manistee, sat an unpretentious building nestled in among others in the business district and built on the bank partly overlooking the river. The front opening of the building had doors and windows facing the street with a wooden sidewalk, and the rear overlooked the water. Prior to 1869, the building was occupied on one side by a news depot and stationery store, and on the other side was a shoe shop.

In the latter half of 1869, the section where the news depot and stationery store existed became occupied by two men, George Vanderpool and Herbert Field, who established a banking firm: Vanderpool & Field.

Herbert Field

Twenty-one-year-old Herbert Field was the son of Stephen Field, formerly of Lewiston, Maine. In his early childhood, he had several narrow escapes from losing his life. Three times he was saved from drowning and was drawn from rivers by his rescuers by the hair on his head. Once he prematurely discharged a rifle while loading it, and it nearly cost him his eyes and his life. Another time he narrowly escaped a fire near his bed when he was sleeping.

At age thirteen, in 1861, he left his home in Lewiston and eventually joined a Maine regiment encamped near Richmond, Virginia. Too young to participate in the war, he borrowed money from a soldier and returned home

Herbert Field. *From* History of Manistee County.

George Vanderpool. *From* History of Manistee County.

to Maine and worked as a newsboy until the sum was paid back. He then found work on a government transport ship carrying supplies to the Union army in New Orleans.

After his return home from that adventure, at the age of fifteen, he sailed from Boston on a ship called *John Tucker* bound on a South American and European voyage. On this journey, he was harshly treated and nearly starved. Near Cape Horn, the ship encountered a terrific storm that lasted for fifteen days, requiring all on board to engage in an almost superhuman effort to survive the cold, hunger and exhaustion.

Following this voyage, Herbert desperately desired to leave the *John Tucker*, but the captain refused to release him. On another voyage, which took him to San Francisco, he escaped, was thrown in jail for being a runaway and was returned to the *John Tucker*.

He eventually found an escape from the ship by joining the navy, where he served aboard the U.S. flagship *Lancaster* for nine months, visiting many South American cities. When he left the *Lancaster*, he joined an English ship bound for Liverpool and on that journey traveled to Ireland, Scotland and Russia. While in the Baltic Sea, the ship wrecked near Riga, Latvia, and he lost the total sum of $180 in gold he had saved on his voyages, along with all of his clothing. In time he was taken in charge by the consul, sent to London and successfully arranged transport back to Boston.

He then attended school at Auburn Commercial College in New York and, following this, moved to New York to find work. Finding none, he joined another ship bound for the Caribbean, returning home in the autumn. He next wrote a lecture on his travels to South America and began delivering it at local colleges.

A fifty-five-year-old woman, Rachael Hill, heard his lecture and was impressed. She offered to aid Herbert by funding his education, which he accepted. Herbert attended the Edward Little Institute but soon abandoned the classes due to poor health.

In December 1868, he met George Vanderpool, and the two decided to enter the banking business together in Manistee, Michigan. Herbert received the financial backing of several thousand dollars from Miss Hill, who now styled herself as his "aunt" in social circles.

George Vanderpool

George Vanderpool was born in the state of New York and was twenty-eight years old when he met Herbert Field. In his early life, he grew up on a farm and received a modest education. In the later 1850s, he made his way to Michigan, where he engaged in lumbering occupations along the western shore around Muskegon and earned the goodwill of his employers. He enlisted during the Civil War and reputably served three years in the Third Michigan Infantry. After mustering out of the army, he returned to Muskegon, working as a clerk in various stores.

In 1868, he met Herbert Field on a trip to New York, and they decided to form a partnership in the banking business. Herbert had the financial backing from Rachael Hill, and George brought the connections in the Muskegon area, where people had known him for over fourteen years by that time. Additionally, he brought along another investor, an S.R. Sanford, who contributed $2,200 to their initial business establishment.

The First Bank of Manistee

In early December 1868, George Vanderpool and Herbert Field chose Manistee as the town to establish their new bank and opened the First Bank of Manistee. Their business was located in the previously described two-story building. The adjoining business on the main floor was a shoe shop, and upstairs was a dentist office.

George also brought the experience of the banking business to the partnership from his years as a clerk, along with business connections in Muskegon, and Herbert provided capital and worldly experience. Arriving in Manistee ahead of Herbert, George rented a two-story house near their selected bank building, where he and his newly married wife, Helen, resided.

Herbert joined George in Manistee in February 1869, and within a month of his arrival, he came to know every nook of the small town. He easily made the acquaintance of strangers and was always cheerful and pleasant, with a good word for everyone when he saw them.

Perhaps the only fault anyone ever attributed to Herbert as a businessman was that he was often guilty of telling too much about his business. He displayed money in his possession constantly, and some regarded him as thoughtless and inexperienced in doing so.

The capital of the new bank was not large, but George was successful in obtaining interest from the nearby town of Muskegon and made dealings to build up their business. The firm developed a good reputation guided by the two young men, which was a credit to their industry. As they conducted their business, after a year, they were really gaining a strong hold within the community.

Disappearance

While Herbert was younger than George, and had the appearance sometimes of a youthful figure living with his adopted aunt, both men made many friends, which externally added gradual strength to their firm. Both were affable and friendly within the community, so it came as somewhat of a shock on the morning of September 6, 1869, when word got out that Herbert was missing and was supposed to have run away. News spread rapidly through the small town.

The story soon emerged that Herbert had broken away from the restraint of his adopted aunt and sought freedom in flight. While these rumors were in circulation, Miss Hill was protesting the allegations, expressing concerns that Herbert was the victim of foul play.

Together with these rumors, several leading citizens raised concerns that the firm's funds, over $2,000, were left in the safe at Willard Hall & Company, rather than on the premises of Vanderpool & Field. Repeated inquires of George about Herbert's whereabouts only brought out his opinion that Herbert had run away. Investigations into this theory could yield no outward reason why Herbert would do so.

Friends, believing it was all a misunderstanding, speculated Herbert probably left on the steamer on the night of Sunday, September 5, scheduled to return on Tuesday. When Tuesday came and Herbert did not arrive, no relief was brought to the growing concerns. Where was Herbert?

More active measures were then taken to try to locate Herbert Field. Citizens set up watches on the bank and also on the house of George Vanderpool. On early Wednesday morning, September 8, George was observed to be cleaning inside the bank. Those observing him were determined to find out why. Enlisting the sheriff, they accompanied him to the bank to examine the interior in the presence of George Vanderpool.

Up until this point, George had ignored the suspicions and rumors that he had something to do with Herbert's disappearance. When the sheriff entered the bank with a party of citizens, he knew for sure things were escalating. Under pressure from the community, the sheriff took him into custody. Following advice of his attorney, George cooperated, even though no warrant had been issued for his arrest.

George maintained his innocence, and even the sheriff—who was interviewed later—expressed a belief that he was. Telegraphs spread all over the state that a banker was in jail suspected of murdering his partner. During this time, the community at large could not be convinced George was guilty, and close friends vocally asserted his innocence. Though inside the walls of the jail, George had liberty to move about within and shared the hospitality of his jailer's table, where they kept him abreast of the developments in the investigation.

The Search

While George remained incarcerated, the investigation accelerated with a search in every direction from Manistee to ascertain the whereabouts of Herbert Field, whether living or dead. The sheriff offered a $300 reward for a dead body and a $50 reward if he was found alive or information on his whereabouts. Soon the $300 reward was increased to $500 when other members of the community added to it.

As the days continued, the public opinion began to shift toward George Vanderpool, as more and more seemingly circumstantial evidence against him mounted. Still, there was no body.

The Manistee River was dragged; local buildings were searched along with Lake Manistee. The search then began up the shoreline of Lake Michigan,

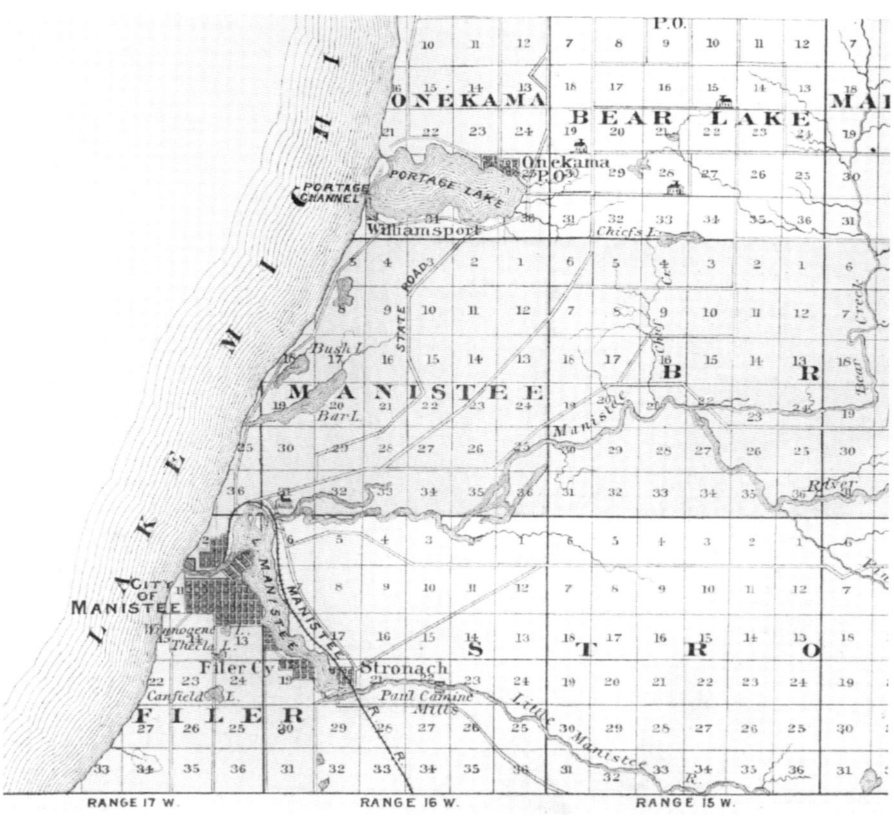

Map of Manistee, 1882. *From* History of Manistee County.

in either direction, combing the beaches. By the following Sunday, search efforts had begun to wane, and little was done except by a few private individuals using pike poles on the river bottom, inserting them into the sand along the beaches.

During the second week of his arrest, George became impatient, desiring to be released to attend to his business. Following advice from counsel, he agreed to withhold demands for release until the authorities had satisfied themselves and discharged him.

Fears mounted that George's attorney would gain his release by a writ of habeas corpus, and so convinced were some that a murder had been committed, a complaint to the court was made on Friday, September 17, in the afternoon to legally charge George Vanderpool with the murder of Herbert Field.

A warrant was accordingly issued by the court and delivered to the sheriff, with a community still torn in two over the mystery.

Little did anyone know, within a few hours, a larger enigma would soon unfold.

FOUND

The body of Herbert Field was found twenty-eight miles north by a man named Rollin O'Crispin near Frankfort, cast ashore on the beach of Lake Michigan. Wounds on the head showed every indication of blunt force trauma. There was a rope encircling his neck, as if it had been used to weigh the body down in some deeper water and broken loose. The body had apparently been discarded in the Manistee River or taken in a boat down the river to Lake Michigan.

When this news was received, it forever settled the fact that Herbert had been murdered at the hand of an assassin. After a coroner's inquest was held at the scene where his body was found, the deceased was carried onboard the steamer *J. Barber* and conveyed to Manistee. Once the ship arrived in the harbor, it was placed in a warehouse and authorities notified.

On Saturday morning came the chilling news, striking at the heart of the community, as word spread not only in Manistee but across the telegraph lines in the state as well. Herbert Field was dead, and he had been cruelly murdered.

VANDERPOOL INDICTED

Up until the discovery of the body, George Vanderpool had great confidence and expressed the belief that Herbert was still alive and out in the great wide world somewhere. With Herbert's extensive travel experiences, it was indeed a plausible theory.

When news of the discovery of his body came, the sheriff had great difficulty convincing George that it was true. He initially exhibited levity toward the idea when it was made known to him, such was his disbelief.

Once he was satisfied they were telling him the truth, he manifested a great expression of love and respect for his murdered partner and he wanted to see the remains. The state of public feeling about him being let out to see it caused the sheriff to deny this request.

The coroner's jury was held inside the bank building all day on Saturday, and by six o'clock in the evening, they had rendered the following verdict:

> *That the body is the body of Herbert Field: that he came to his death on the 5th of September, A.D. 1869, in the building lately occupied by Vanderpool and Field for banking purposes, in the city of Manistee, by being struck upon the head in two places with some blunt instrument or weapon, used willfully and maliciously by George Vanderpool for the purpose of murdering him, the said Herbert Field.*

The verdict was drawn up under the supervision of the prosecuting attorney of the county as an *ex-parte* proceeding, with no power to affect the legal rights of George Vanderpool.

Following this, George Vanderpool was arraigned before the justice of the peace, and waiving his right to a preliminary hearing, he was charged with murder and a trial date was scheduled.

BUILDING A CASE

From that time forward to the date of the trial, the prosecuting attorney diligently engaged in preserving and collecting testimony to build a case against George Vanderpool.

During George's imprisonment at the jail, his wife, Helen, was allowed to see him but permitted only to talk with him through a hole in the wooden door of his cell. For a brief moment, the sheriff considered she might have in some way knowledge of the crime, but soon after questioning her, he was satisfied she knew nothing of the matter.

On October 1, the sheriff received a letter from George Vanderpool's mother, addressed to George. She had been reading the newspaper articles about him and wrote him to tell him if he had indeed taken Herbert Field's life, whatever the facts might be, that he should make a full confession.

On October 3, George Vanderpool wrote a long letter in response to her, some thirty-eight pages. Some highlights of that letter are as follows:

> *My Dear, Dear Mother,*
>
> *Oh tell me, have I yet a friend? This is a beautiful Sabbath morning. I am seated in my cell, in jail, for the dark and bloody crime of murder....*
>
> *O how I could talk if you were here, but what use to write, when it will come so far short of my feelings. But I will try to answer a few things....*
>
> *You ask me to write, "truthfully, faithfully, a statement for God and man to read." You ask it by my hope of heaven and earth, etc. I can do that and call God the spirit of poor, poor Herbert to bear witness, yet this is scoffed at as mockery and my very innocence is called impudence, but, oh thanks be to God, He knows. He knows, feeling that I am ready to go, ready now and can go smiling at the world's mistake.*
>
> *I leave it to God and time to prove.*
>
> *Now my more than mother, I am to close this and say farewell, but first let me say this: "Rest easy as to me. I am content, God's will be done, not mine. My heart is right. You have been a true and noble woman a guide in my life, and I love you for it, and God will reward you for it."*
>
> *You may freely bet your soul on my innocence, and when the people tell you George Vanderpool was a murderer, say to them "you never knew him."*
>
> *If I die for this crime I will not be the first nor yet the last, that have suffered unjustly. Let us hope in God. Remember me kindly...and may Heaven bless and protect you....*
>
> *Now as ever,*
> *George Vanderpool*

Of course, this letter was copied and given to the prosecution as well as the defense. Similar letters were gathered by both sides and witnesses interviewed.

Arraignment

On December 22, 1869, George Vanderpool was brought before the Circuit Court for the County of Manistee and arraigned for the crime of murder. By this time, the general citizenship of Manistee seemed satisfied he was guilty and eagerly awaited the coming court date to try to convict him. At the same time, there were many who felt that George could hardly do such a deed and were anxious for more light to be shed on the subject.

On the day of the arraignment, a vast concourse of citizens gathered to witness the event, packing the courtroom to its utmost capacity. Many who gathered had never seen Vanderpool, and many more had not seen him since he was last quietly engaged in his business as a banker. By this time, the man had been imprisoned for three months, and now he was charged with murder. An estimated five hundred people had gathered inside and outside of the courtroom to satisfy their curiosity.

George Vanderpool, the prisoner, walked up the long aisle of the courtroom, densely packed with people on both sides, with many in the room unable to see him progress on his journey until he arrived at the prisoner's chair and the sheriff unshackled the irons from his wrists.

If someone had walked in a few moments later, they might have mistaken the genteel man standing beside the chair as an attorney, such was his appearance and dress. He wore a fine black suit, spotless linen, fitted gloves and a glossy silk hat, which stood out in contrast to the position he occupied in the room.

At the proper time, he arose and listened to the reading of the charge from the prosecuting attorney with calmness and self-composure. Despite this, it was not difficult to detect beneath the seemingly smooth surface an uneasiness within. Upon hearing the charge, standing by his attorney, George Vanderpool pleaded "not guilty."

First Trial

The following day, a motion was made for continuance until the next term of the court, on the account of lack of material witnesses for the defense. The public concern at this legal maneuver was that the trial would be delayed too long and evidence might be lost; as a result the prisoner might be discharged—not because of innocence, but because of a technicality.

The judge of the Circuit Court, J.G. Ramsdell, however, denied the continuance but granted the defense a delay for one month to give them an opportunity to procure their witnesses. The trial began on February 1 and lasted through February 24, 1870, during a typical cold winter in Michigan. Thirteen days were consumed by presenting evidence and the final six days by summing up to the jury the case by counsel.

Throughout the trial, George remained very composed. He was permitted some liberty in the courtroom, being allowed to sit near his counsel quietly advising him, but also allowed to stand near the stove to warm himself, as well as write at a writing desk and pass notes to his attorney during the progress of the trial. He was even at times allowed to sit near his wife and console her.

George would occasionally banter with members of the audience in a social manner. One audience member remarked to him that the end of the trial would come before long, and George replied, "Yes, and so will Christmas." One day during the trial, George was walking into the courtroom beside an insurance man who was discussing business with a customer, and he asked him, "How much will you charge to ensure my liberty?" The man replied, "One hundred percent."

Throughout the trial, if an attempt can be made to describe his conduct, it perhaps would serve as a case study scrutinized by legal scholars. The entire case was entirely founded heavily on circumstantial evidence. George would express his opinion about the incorrectness of testimony to his counsel but for the most part remained calm, composed and seemingly attendant throughout the trial. However, his lightness of attitude, confidence and occasional smiling probably worked against him in the eyes of the jury.

Testimony

During the trial, there was a considerable amount of testimony given. Witnesses for the prosecution presented a story of the bank not doing as well as outward appearance suggested. Witnesses included a bookkeeper who handled money for Vanderpool and Field and a courier who delivered money from their office to Miss Hill. All of this was to demonstrate inconsistencies in the ledger sheets that were challenged as having been altered at various times.

There was another expert witness, Wesley Horton, a fisherman in the Manistee River for over twelve years, who testified on the strength of the current and the speed in which objects would travel in the water. He was on the water on September 5, 1869, the day Field went missing, and recalled the waters were quite heavy that day from the weather. Another fisherman, A.C. Taggart, testified to a southward current that was strong that day.

There was a witness named R.G. Peters who testified to driving past the bank in his buggy the day after Field went missing, and he stopped to ask George if he knew where he was. He stated that George thought Field had run away, taking some valuable papers, mentioning three specific notes.

Other people who had spoken with George in the days that followed mentioned he thought Field had taken another trip on the salt water again, as he had done in the past. In all cases, George indicated he was only speculating and did not know where he had gone.

A barber, George Woodruff, whose store was across the street, testified to having seen Field earlier in the day he had gone missing but not in the evening, when he usually went home.

Other witnesses came from those members of the coroner's jury who investigated the bank premises. They introduced the discovery of a missing section of carpet in the bank that was cut without reference to the seams and discovering reddish spots on the floor below. They had concluded that it might have been blood. When they lifted other sections of the carpet, they found some other spots that they thought was also blood. The defense presented witnesses that stated they saw George have a nosebleed at the bank.

VERDICT

On February 25, 1870, the jury went into deliberation, following a three-hour final statement by George Vanderpool, which was considered a most remarkable effort in points of ability, candor and manner of delivery in proclaiming his innocence. Six hours later, they returned with a verdict of "guilty of murder in the first degree."

An awful silence followed the statement by the jury foreman, broken by a wail of agony from the broken heart of Helen Vanderpool, who collapsed into her husband's arms. George Vanderpool was now branded a murderer.

The next morning, on February 26, George was arraigned for sentencing. In a clear, unbroken voice, in his final statements to the judge, which lasted for about ten long minutes, he maintained he had told the truth and was innocent of the crime. In the latter part of his address, his voice quivered and broke and was overcome by emotions. It was a solemn and impressive scene and brought tears to the eyes of many in the audience.

One such witness commented: "It was a sad and pitiful scene, to see one in the flower of young manhood, surrounded with so many things to make life precious and attractive, thus untimely consigned to a living tomb."

George was sentenced to life in the Michigan State Penitentiary in Jackson in solitary confinement. On Sunday, February 27, at eleven o'clock at night, the sheriff quietly took his prisoner in a two-horse sleigh, accompanied by only a neighbor, over one hundred miles of forest and field to Muskegon. There he was placed on a train to Jackson.

A Letter from George

On the train to Jackson, George Vanderpool wrote a letter in response to an inquiry from an editor of a newspaper:

> *Mr. Turner, Editor of the* Grand Rapids Eagle*:*
>
> *I am seated on the cars on my way to Jackson. The hour is near when I am to say farewell to this beautiful world and God's loving sunlight, and shall be entombed in a living tomb.*
>
> *You asked me today if I thought I had a fair trial. I don't remember my reply. Will say it may be fair in the eyes of some—but I am not satisfied, as the same assistance was not granted me as was granted the people.*
>
> *They had at their command all the talent of the legal profession, a united and enthusiastic people, and the county treasurer to pay the bills, while I had not a dollar to bring distant witnesses, and people are slow to give aid or evidence in an unpopular cause.*
>
> *With that same aid I cannot but feel that my case would appear different. I here, too, remember that the jury was taken from that same people; that they have rendered a verdict, and I must abide the law, and say farewell*

to all that is near and dear—to all that makes life desirable. And branded with a dishonor worse than death, I leave this world in the prime of life, yet an innocent man.
George Vanderpool

The Second Trial

Immediately upon close of the trial, George Vanderpool's attorney filed an appeal for a new trial. Soon after, a public meeting was called in Muskegon and a committee of sixteen people appointed to raise funds to secure material aid to defray the expenses of a new trial and hire new attorneys.

The press and the citizens of the surrounding communities took sides, and the region became divided over this case.

The result of this effort was that a request for a new trial was granted and scheduled eight months later for October 1870. This time, the venue was moved to Kalamazoo County. The presiding judge was Charles R. Brown of the Kalamazoo Circuit Court.

George Vanderpool was released from solitary confinement at the penitentiary in Jackson and transferred to a jail in Kalamazoo in May. As soon as it was known that he was in the jail in Kalamazoo, large numbers of people crowded to see him. His excitement and joy over this partial delivery to freedom was intense.

During the second trial, which lasted over a month, new testimony was entered that shed a different light on the case. The funds raised for George Vanderpool's defense enabled them to hire John Van Arman, perhaps the best-known attorney in the state of Michigan at the time.

The defense revealed George Vanderpool had been sick the day leading up to Field disappearing and was taking medicine from the apothecary in town. George had been challenged while in jail the night the body was found on what weapon he had used to hit Field on the head, and he said he had not struck Field and could not have, as he was very sick that day.

Finally, Rachael Hill testified to the living arrangements she had with Herbert Field and having seen him leave the house that morning, and she described what he was wearing. She said Herbert told her he was going to the bank to write some letters and had not come home for lunch or supper, and she recalled mentioning it to a neighbor.

She also said that George and his wife had paid her a visit the day after Field went missing, and there was a disagreement on the amounts of money in the ledgers. Rachael suggested Field had an amount of $7,000 in the bank the night he went missing, and George dismissed this, indicating it was no more than $700 or $800.

Rachael also testified that a few days before he had been killed, she saw Field with a handful of foreign gold coins.

The prosecution's case in the second trial again centered on circumstantial evidence and eyewitness testimony. Their case contained a witness who claimed to see a man in a boat on the Manistee River on the evening Field went missing. They introduced another witness who saw George Vanderpool that evening lighting a lamp in the office, and later, he was seen wearing different clothes when he visited a friend's house, all within an eighty-five-minute period or so when Field went missing.

The defense, however, was able to present on cross-examination an argument that the timeline suggested by the prosecution was impossible within the time suggested. They demonstrated the amount of time it would have taken to walk to the bank of the river with a body, to load a body into a boat, secure it with an anchor, as was alleged, be seen on the river in the boat at the time he was supposed to have been identified, and dispose of it.

Then George would have had to row back, against the current, which was already confirmed by multiple fisherman to be strong that evening, bring the boat back on shore, stow it away, as no boat was ever discovered on the shore disturbed from its location that evening. Then he would have had to make it to his office, change clothes after lighting the lamp, and ultimately be seen at the neighbor's house at the allotted time he was. When all added up, it would have required 120 minutes, even with a conservative estimate.

Finally, new evidence was presented that incontestably demonstrated that Herbert Field was seen alive after George Vanderpool had left the bank at noon.

When all of these facts were demonstrated, and aligned with the witness testimony, it decimated the prosecution's proposed eighty-five-minute timeline of events.

At the conclusion of that trial, the outcome was a deadlocked jury. Of the twelve jurors, seven voted for conviction and five firmly for acquittal. Unable to agree on a verdict, the result was a mistrial.

The Third Trial

The following year, in August 1871, a new trial was held. This time, the venue was moved to Barry County. Approximately one hundred jurymen were summoned, from which the jury was selected.

The same material was argued by both sides, with even more vigor. This trial had a different outcome. On September 19, 1871, after another four-week-long proceeding, the jury returned to the courtroom with a verdict of not guilty. Helen Vanderpool gave a scream that the newspapers said no language could describe. George sat for a moment or two, stunned, and then turned his eyes upward, giving thanks for his deliverance.

The lengthy saga of multiple trials became known as the Great Vanderpool Murder Trial across the state of Michigan. George returned to the world, released into the arms of his wife and family. He continued his financial pursuits and lived the rest of his days as a free man.

On Sunday, October 8, 1871, a massive fire leveled a broad swath of Michigan and Wisconsin, including the cities of Peshtigo, Holland and Manistee. The wood buildings in Manistee were the first to go up in flames, with over half of the structures in the village lost. The town slowly recovered and was rebuilt in brick.

Following his acquittal, George and Helen moved to Ohio and had two children. They eventually moved back to New York. George passed away at the age of eighty in 1922, and Helen passed away in 1925 at the age of seventy-eight.

Was George truly innocent of the great crime charged against him? Or was he a man who successfully got away with murder? Defense attorney John Van Arman pointed out in the second trial that during the first two days when Field went missing, no one assumed he was murdered. Then rumors circulated on the third day and began to spread around Manistee, and Vanderpool was targeted as the one and only culprit, without examining any other possible suspects. This was a week before the body was found on September 17. Was this a case of blind mob justice convicting an innocent man?

As with any murder case, looking back 150 years, it is always compelling to consider the question: If George Vanderpool was indeed innocent, then who really killed Herbert Field?

Review of all the material brings to light two other possible suspects who were ignored during the investigation.

The Shoemaker?

First, there was the shoemaker, a Mr. Canavan, who had the business adjacent to the office of the First Bank of Manistee held by Vanderpool and Field.

He was reported to have testified to historians later that his firsthand knowledge of the night's events when Herbert Field went missing was not included in the investigation, nor did he mention this at trial. In fact, when he did testify, he indicated he had been in and about both buildings on Sunday and did not see anything unusual.

He later claimed, outside of the courtroom, that on the night Field went missing, both Herbert Field and George Vanderpool came over to his shop and asked him and another occupant in the store to witness some legal documents. When they had signed the documents, Field and Vanderpool left, returning to their office. Later, Canavan said he heard loud noises as if they were wrestling, and he assumed it was Field playing with his dog.

As he locked up for the night soon after, he went by the front door of the two young men's office, after hearing the noises again, and rapped on the window to tell them to quiet down. He claimed he looked in the window, which had a shade covering most of the glass, and could not see anyone inside. He said the noises stopped after he called out, so he went home.

If this was true, then why was he not allowed to testify at trial? One would think the prosecution would want to know this. Especially when Canavan later learned that Field's dog was tied up at home that evening and not with him in the office.

One could speculate that he knew more or made up the story to give himself cover to divert attention to Vanderpool. Did he have something to do with Field's death? After all, Field was hit with a blunt weapon. Could that have been a shoemaker's hammer? The object he was struck with was never identified or presented at trial.

What About Miss Hill?

The other suspect who seemed to avoid scrutiny was Miss Rachael Hill, the benefactor whom Field referred to as his adopted aunt. She had a financial interest in the firm through Herbert, and if the business was not doing so well, this might have been a motive for her to assault the man to whom she had loaned the money.

Following the first trial of George Vanderpool, she purchased a small house on the north side of the river in Manistee and lived there entirely alone. She was regarded by those who knew her as an eccentric person, and she never married.

In personal appearance, she was described as prepossessing, and it was said she became a benefactor of Field through a freak friendship. Perhaps there was more going on with this relationship than was known? Could she have also been a rejected lover? Was she lying on the witness stand about the amounts of money she claimed to have seen Herbert Field with? No one else seemed to be able to corroborate her statements on this.

Further, it was discovered that in the latter part of her life, she claimed to be a sufferer of neuralgia and on that account was in the habit of taking morphine freely. She likely was addicted to this during the time she spent with Field.

Several years after the trial, a Dr. Ellis in the Manistee community was driving his carriage past her house and noticed that the curtains were drawn, and the doorstep had not been swept from recently fallen snow.

He decided to make a welfare check on Miss Hill, knocking on the front door. When no answer came, he tried the knob and found it fastened. He subsequently went to a window and peered inside. There he discovered her dead, lying in her bed, with an empty bottle on her nightstand. She had taken a fatal dose of morphine, sinking into the sleep that knows no waking.

Did Field dissolve his partnership with Vanderpool because of her? Did she have a falling out with him that compelled him to do this? Could it be she struck him in anger, causing his death, and then disposed of his body in the river?

After the devastating fire in Manistee, the case faded into memory as the town faced the challenge of rebuilding, and the mysterious death of Herbert Field was forgotten in the spirit of the woods.

4

UNFATHOMABLE MYSTERY

THE MORRIS MURDERS (1879)

May God's hatred rest upon the beastly perpetrator of this most horrible deed, and speed the time when his smitten conscience will cause him to cry out the confession of his own guilt.

—The Niles Democrat, *October 4, 1879*

On the night of September 28, 1879, thirty-two-year-old Charles Henry Morris and his wife, twenty-nine-year-old Esther Morris, had just completed a long day. They were returning from a Sunday afternoon of calling on the homes of their friends Peter Moon and John Gould and later the Kern family in Porter Township, Michigan. The topic of discussion among their friends consisted of the anticipation of a promising harvest as well as catching up on social news of the region.

They arrived home around seven o'clock and were anticipating a restful evening. Unbeknownst to the young couple, concealed in the darkness that fateful night lay the proverbial serpent with no pity for the damned.

First Settler

Charles was the youngest son of Dolphin and Nancy Morris. His father was the first white settler in Van Buren County in 1829, and he surveyed the early roads in the Little Prairie Ronde area.

Dolphin Morris had established a prosperous 320-acre farm, where he raised a family of four boys and two girls, giving each of them a small farm as they reached maturity. The Morris family was well known in the county. Most of his sons' land was in Volinia Township, and his own farm was just over the line in Decatur Township just west of Swift Lake.

Dolphin Morris. *From* History of Van Buren County.

Esther was the daughter of Asa Jones of Edwardsburg, in Cass County. Charles and Esther were married on December 24, 1869.

Charles was still living in the original family house when his father passed away in 1870, leaving the property to him and his mother. His mother transferred the last of the estate to him when she died in 1877, leaving Charles as the sole owner of the original family farm.

In March, one year later, the couple had a baby boy they named Frankie. For a time, sunshine returned to their home. However, their joy was short-lived, as their infant son passed away abruptly in September.

Nancy Morris. *From* History of Van Buren County.

Charles and Esther resided now in the lonely homestead, working the farm. A young girl, Jennie Bull, who was a domestic worker, lived upstairs. Despite their recent history of loss and tragedy, the couple still kindled optimism in the wake of despair when looking toward their future.

Their house was set back sixty rods from the main road, and their land was partially forested amid cultivated fields. The land was fertile, and Charles had sowed most of the available open land with crops. With favorable weather conditions that season, the yields had been quite large.

Despite their dedication to the land and the remoteness of their property in the southeast corner of Decatur Township, the couple maintained quite a large circle of friends. Sundays, as with many farmers in this area, became a time for prayer at the house of worship followed by visits to neighbors and socializing.

Dark Clouds of the Shylock

Charles and Esther were feeling optimistic at this time for reasons that went well beyond the success of their crops. Since his mother's death, leading up to the weeks prior to this September evening, Charles had endured a sinister threat of another kind that unsettled the harmony of their comfortable home.

A dark bearded, money-lending shylock of a man named Milo D. Matteson had ingratiated himself with the good-natured Charles following Charles's mother's passing and secured a mortgage on the farm. A short time later, Matteson sought to collect on the mortgage in the amount of ten times what was agreed to.

On hearing of this deceit, Charles Morris declared the mortgage was a forgery, and a lawsuit between the two men began. The Matteson-Morris legal battle in the courts was quite a sensation in the community. It also created a lot of stress for Esther, who became ill with fever in her postpartum depression at one point during the conflict.

Charles H. Morris. *From* History of Van Buren County.

Charles gained assistance from his brothers with the legal expenses. Although the litigation lasted several years, the lower courts ultimately ruled in his favor. The case was then appealed by Matteson to the U.S. District Court in Grand Rapids to be heard in October.

Despite this, Charles held firm to the spirit of optimism that vindication was approaching with a favorable ending. The dark clouds that filled their lives appeared to be clearing. For the first time, on this cool September evening after a successful growing season, the couple was feeling again that the future was indeed bright and promising.

In spite of all of their recent legal troubles, Charles Morris was considered by all who knew him as one of the best men you could come to know. Esther was well educated and known for her pleasant and often cheerful disposition. She was also possessed of splendid business acumen and aided her husband greatly in all of his dealings. The couple was not known or thought to have any enemies, despite the recent court cases that created a sensation.

A KILLER AT NIGHT

In their employ for six years, Jennie Bull resided in an upstairs room in the Morris home. That Sunday she was gone most of the day. Returning home in the evening just before the Morrises' arrived, she entered the house by way of a ladder through a chamber window, something she was accustomed to doing. She later served the Morrises an evening meal around eight o'clock and retired to her upstairs room about a half hour later.

Charles and Esther would soon follow, making their way to their own bedroom on the main floor around nine o'clock. It had been a long day traveling in their buggy across the countryside, and the couple was ready for some much-needed rest.

Within the first hour after lying down for the night, Charles was rousted from bed by the sound of someone opening the front door near the kitchen. Outside, the windmill turned slightly in the breeze, making an occasional clinking sound that interrupted the still of the night. Without stopping to put on his pants, he picked them up with one hand from a nearby chair and went to investigate.

Esther A. Jones Morris. *From* History of Van Buren County.

When Charles arrived at the front door, it was wide open. It is speculated he saw no one there but may have heard a sound outside. Startled out of an early slumber, and perhaps not yet fully regaining his senses, he ventured outside.

Hiding near the house in the shadows a man waited, holding a pistol. When Charles stepped out onto the porch to investigate, the killer pulled the trigger. The bullet passed through his heart and struck the wall next to the front door. Charles collapsed immediately.

The man approached his limp body, leaned over and placed the muzzle close to his face and fired again. This shot left a ring of gunpowder blown into Charles's cheek, with the bullet angling downward, entering the right side of his neck and lodging against his spine. Following this, the shooter stepped over his lifeless body and entered the home.

Awakened by the sound of gunshots, Esther grabbed a revolver stowed in a drawer in their bedroom. Perhaps, after realizing her husband had left her bedside, she intended to rush to his aid, fearing he was in trouble. Instead, she encountered the killer as he made his way through the dining room, heading in her direction. He quickly fired a shot, which passed through her body and ricocheted off the wall. Still on her feet, Esther retreated back into the bedroom and entered an adjoining closet.

The man with the gun pursued her, following the trail of blood left behind during her retreat, aimed and shot her again. This bullet passed through the flesh of her left arm and into a chest of drawers.

At the furthest end of the inside of her closet, she collapsed against the back wall and slowly sank to the floor. The killer followed her, firing his fifth shot, as she slid down to lie prostrate inside the enclosure. He fired yet again, striking her in the breast at such a short range that her nightdress caught fire and burned a large hole. With a revolver in her hand, Esther died in the closet, never returning fire on her attacker.

Having accomplished what he came to do, the killer retreated from the home. On his way out, he spotted the pair of pants lying beside Charles. Picking them up, he carried them with him as he exited. Making his way to the barn, he discarded the pants on a manure heap within.

Inside, he selected a horse, a light bay about seven years old. It was described as having three white feet, a bald face and two watch eyes. These unique blue eyes and markings made this horse easily identifiable to most anyone in the county. It was the fleetest of the Morris's horses, and it had been Esther's personal pride and joy. The killer saddled the horse and rode away.

He was met on the county road leading away from the farm about quarter to ten that evening by a young man named Frank Rosewarne who lived just east of the Morris farm. Frank was returning from a concert at the Sabbath School. Recognizing Esther's horse in the dark as it passed him, he did not see the face of the man riding. The rider, who appeared to be wearing a mask, passed him at an unusually brisk rate of speed—thus Frank assumed he had been mistaken in his identification of the horse. He only realized late the next day, when the news broke about the crime, that he had witnessed the killer making his escape.

Discovery

The murder was not discovered until six o'clock Monday morning, when Jennie Bull came down from upstairs to find Charles Morris shot dead on the front porch. Immediately alarmed by the gruesome scene, she ran down the road in the direction of the neighbor's farm, screaming "Murder!" every few steps. When Jennie was interviewed several hours later, she recounted her discovery, telling investigators that she had slept through the night and never heard any gunshots.

Another hired man, John Klinger, who lived three-quarters of a mile away, had arrived for work shortly after Jennie departed and headed into the barn to feed the horses. He missed encountering Jennie on the road, as he arrived from the opposite direction. Upon discovering that Esther Morris's horse was gone and the barn door open, he paused and looked about him.

He then observed Morris's pants lying on the manure pile. Deciding to go to the house to notify them about the missing horse and inquire about the pants, he discovered Morris lying on the porch. Initially, he attempted to pick him up but then observed the blood and laid him back down. John took flight, breaking into a desperate run in the opposite direction toward another farm, also crying, "Murder!"

John and Jennie's cries for help were heard across the nearby fields. Soon neighbors were aroused from farms in every direction and flocked to see Charles lying in a pool of blood. Elias Morris, Charles's older brother, and his wife were among the first to arrive. It was not long after that Elias discovered Esther Morris's body inside the closet. The disturbing spectacle of the woman shot so many times sparked terror and outrage.

When authorities were called to the scene, they were dismayed at the lack of the appearance of a motive. Stealing money or jewelry was soon ruled out, as in the very bedroom where Esther Morris was found lay an unfastened drawer in the dresser bureau with over two hundred dollars, two valuable gold watches and a massive lady's solid gold chain. There was also at least one hundred dollars sitting in plain sight on the top of the dresser, untouched. It was later learned that Morris had just sold one thousand bushels of wheat a few days before. He was said to be scheduled to take another load on that Monday. Additionally, money was found undisturbed inside one of his pockets in the pair of pants that had been discarded in the barn.

Rumors

Later that same morning, the bay horse was located in South Bend, Indiana, running free in the streets, abandoned some thirty-five miles from the scene of the murder. The horse was found to be in a jaded condition, as if someone had ridden it hard. It was bareback with no bridle, but there were marks of a saddle having recently been on its back. It was theorized that the rider had either switched to a different horse or boarded a train for Chicago, taking the saddle and tack with him in making his escape.

Theories soon arose as to potential culprits. One was advanced about a disgruntled hired hand named Riley Huntley who had been dismissed from employment by Charles Morris in July. Rumors circulated that this man had sworn vengeance.

Upon investigation, this theory was soon realized to be too flimsy a motive for consideration as both Jennie Bull and John Klinger were interviewed about Huntley, and they claimed he was discharged with no ill feelings toward the Morrises when he left. He even cordially bid them "goodbye" on his departure. Huntley had been caught intoxicated while at work and was remorseful. He had remained there working for two or three days after being discharged and joked and chatted with the Morrises while at work. Charles Morris had brought him to town when he was ready to go home.

It is interesting to note, however, that Huntley moved away to South Bend, Indiana, the very same place where the Morris horse was later discovered. Huntley was located and questioned in South Bend but soon ruled out as a suspect.

Another theory advanced, likely from the same rumor mill, was that the killer was a rejected lover from Esther Morris's past who had come back

Charles H. Morris farm. *From* History of Van Buren County.

to settle a score. This theory, possibly suggested after it was discovered that Esther had been shot four times, twice more than Charles, was also soon dismissed.

The couple had been married since 1869, and on the upcoming Christmas Eve, they would have celebrated their tenth anniversary. Almost a decade had passed since she had even looked at another man as a suitor according to those that knew her, and it was agreed that anyone holding such ardent admiration for her would have long since moved on.

There was, however, another theory that began to take hold as the investigation continued. This one did seem to offer sufficient motive.

Inside the Matteson-Morris Case

The investigation of the crime scene led investigators to realize that the shooter was not a novice. The murders appeared to have been carefully planned to coincide when there were no witnesses. Whoever had done this may have watched the house and prepared in advance, knowing when the hired girl would retire, when the other hired hands went home for the day, the habits of the couple at home and so on. He also seemed to know what parts of the house they would all be in when he approached to make his move.

Thus the belief soon formed that the perpetrator was a skilled assassin who came prepared. He never missed a shot, knew when the couple would be most vulnerable and even selected a fast horse for escape. Was the killer familiar with Charles Morris, knowing how best to lure him outside?

Had he arrived on foot or been brought there by someone else? Had he been observing the comings and goings of the house in stealth? Could he have been given full details by someone else who was familiar with the family? Or was he just a random thug who happened upon the farm looking to steal a horse?

Was this an act of vengeance? Or was this a strategic assassination? There were these and many other questions by those who studied the scene. Most importantly, who would want to kill the couple?

Investigators soon began to look into the recent legal struggle in the Matteson-Morris case.

Back in July 1873, Charles filed a countersuit against Milo Matteson with the court after Matteson entered a claim that a mortgage against the lands of Charles Morris existed in the amount of $11,000 dated April 1872. Matteson affirmed he was the mortgagee. The genuineness of this mortgage was disputed by Charles Morris, who sued to have it canceled.

Soon after, it was discovered there existed three other mortgages on the lands of Amos Morris, his brother, in Cass County, wherein Matteson was also the mortgagee. Amos Morris declared these mortgages were not genuine.

The ultimate outcome was that Matteson was arrested for forgery after a thorough investigation. In January 1874, a long trial was held in the Van Buren County Circuit Court, and Matteson was convicted. A new trial was scheduled shortly after filing of a stay of proceedings. Following this, the venue was changed to St. Joseph County, where Matteson was acquitted.

Matteson then commenced with a suit of foreclosure indicting Amos Morris in the U.S. Court for perjury when he responded negatively to the foreclosure bill. He took the same action against Charles Morris. Both cases were dismissed by the court.

Undaunted, Matteson filed a suit against Amos Morris in the Cass County Circuit Court. Following voluminous testimony, the judge granted a decree for the foreclosures. Amos Morris then appealed the decision to the Michigan Supreme Court, and the mortgages were reviewed and determined to be forgeries. Finally, the fraudulent mortgages against the land of Amos Morris were terminated. Despite the court decisions on the forgeries, Amos did not retaliate and pursue criminal charges against Milo Matteson.

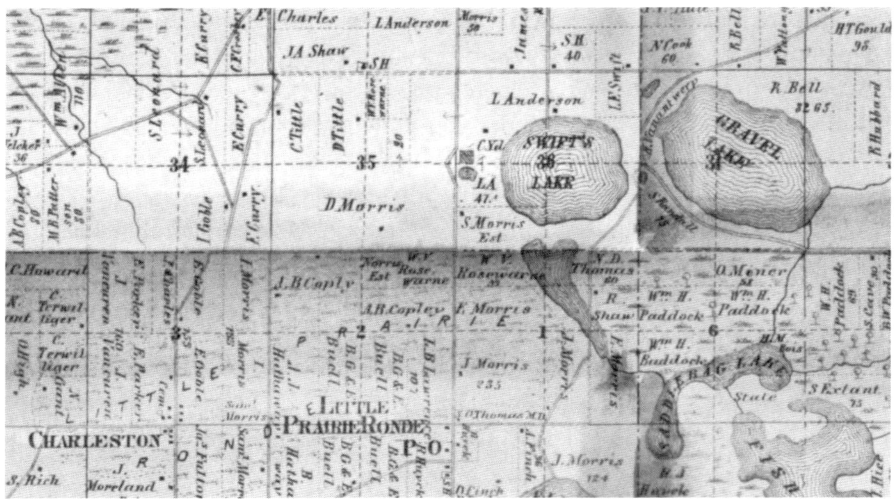

The 1860 Atlas showing the Dolphin Morris farm and Morris family farms. *Library of Congress.*

The foreclosure proceedings against Charles Morris were also challenged and transferred to the U.S. Court in Grand Rapids. They were pending on the upcoming docket for October 1879, when the couple was brutally murdered in their home in September.

In this case, Charles Morris was not disputing the existence of the mortgage but maintaining he never received the funds the mortgage claimed to have disbursed to him. The original mortgage was for $1,100, the amount of funds he claimed was given to him by Matteson. Allegedly, Matteson had forged an additional zero onto the documents, making it appear to be $11,000, and in turn sold it to another party, who then initiated foreclosure when payment in full was disputed.

In the months following the murder, the administrator of Charles Morris's will was his brother Elias Morris. Elias continued the battle in the federal court, using the same attorneys that carried the defense for Amos Morris. Absent the key witnesses in the case, the defense faced a tougher challenge. However, they did have the Michigan Supreme Court's decision on the forgeries by Matteson in the earlier Amos Morris case to present.

During the trial, Milo Matteson was cross-examined by the defense, and they asked him extensively about his whereabouts and movements for the week or two preceding the murder of Charles Morris. This line of questioning made Matteson decidedly uncomfortable on the stand, and his attorney requested an adjournment, which lasted a week.

It was during these several days that Matteson acquiesced and offered to settle the complaint for $2,500 with the administrator of the Morris estate, as well as discontinue the suit and pay his own court costs. There was indeed a legitimate mortgage balance to Matteson but of only $1,200 determined to be owed when settling the estate.

By that point, the court fees and other legal fees of all parties amounted to $40,000. The settlement offer was accepted by Elias Morris and Matteson, and the latter party agreed to release any and all further claims on the estate of Charles Morris.

A History of Fraud

His manipulations with the Morris brothers was not the first time Milo Matteson tried to defraud others using the legal system. One case filed by him against a man named Marks in 1873 went to the Michigan Supreme Court. Matteson was compelled in that final decision to refund the money to him.

An earlier case occurred in 1870 against a man named Caleb M. Gardner who originally borrowed $105 from Matteson. Matteson annually renewed the mortgages on his property until they exceeded $500, despite already receiving full payment on the sum owed. This too went to the Michigan Supreme Court, which ruled in favor of Gardner, granting a refund.

In 1877, Matteson attempted the same tactics with Solomon Steele after he loaned him a small sum of money. Steele grew tired of the games Matteson was playing and forbade him from coming on his property. Matteson in turn arrived with three armed men. One man drew a revolver on Steele.

While the gun was leveled on Steele, Matteson struck him with a sled stake. Steele brought suit against Matteson in the Circuit Court and offered to settle with Matteson for $100. Matteson refused, and the case went to trial. Steele won and was awarded $600 for damages.

A December 1880 edition of the *True Northerner* newspaper in Paw Paw, Michigan, wrote: "If anyone thinks honesty is not the best policy, we would not advise him to prove it by citing Matteson as an illustration."

Following the settlement of the case on the Charles Morris estate, Milo Matteson left Michigan and moved to Chicago.

Unexpected Sleigh Ride

The investigators found it difficult to not consider Milo Matteson a suspect in the murder of Charles and Esther Morris, especially since there was pending litigation with the deceased at the time of the murder. The investigating constable, Warren Botsford, eagerly began to search for a way to connect Matteson to the crime and bring about a conviction.

The Van Buren County Board of Supervisors met in Paw Paw in October and voted to appropriate $2,000 from the budget to defray the cost of expenses in the investigation to find the murderers of Charles and Esther Morris.

Whether following up on a rumor or a personal hunch, Constable Botsford believed a man named Floyd Smith, an overseer on the Matteson farm in Hamilton Township, was involved with Milo Matteson in the murder of the couple. On a wintry night in December, the day after Christmas, Constable Botsford, along with a deputy, arrived at the home of Floyd Smith.

Botsford informed Smith he had a warrant for his arrest. When Smith asked him to read the warrant, Botsford responded, "It would take too long."

Smith then inquired if the people of Decatur believed he had committed the crime, and Botsford assured him that they did. He also told Smith there was a lot of excitement over the matter, and he intended to take him into custody.

Floyd Smith replied that he could prove that he was home all that day and night when the crime took place but made it clear he was willing to go stand trial to prove his innocence. He agreed to accompany the officers into Decatur but asked that some of his neighbors be called over before he went with them, so they could look after his wife and two young children for him in his absence. It was a cold December night, and he wanted to ensure their safety.

Botsford refused to allow this, perhaps believing Floyd intended to take flight. Instead, he placed Floyd in custody and escorted him outside to an awaiting sleigh. The officers then each took a seat on either side of him and directed their team of horses toward Decatur.

The following events were later described by Floyd Smith to a journalist.

The sleigh had not driven far when Floyd saw there was something blocking the road ahead in the darkness. He turned and asked Botsford what it was, and he simply replied, "It is men."

As the sleigh drew closer to the men, Floyd could see they were all wearing masks or covering their faces with cloth. One of the men cried out, "Whoa," whereupon the constable immediately pulled up his team of horses and came to a stop. He then turned and hopped out of the sleigh on one side, and the other accompanying officer did the same on his side.

Puzzled, Floyd sat alone in the sleigh watching the two officers walk away. He was suddenly seized from behind, dragged from the sleigh, stood on his feet and blindfolded. Following this, one of the men struck him and knocked him down.

His abductors loaded him up in the same sleigh that had been occupied by the two officers and drove on. The sleigh rode for a short time and then came to a stop in a secluded area.

Floyd was still blindfolded when the men adjusted a rope around his neck, dragged him out and tossed the other end of the rope over a limb of a tree. They told him that unless he confessed what he knew about the Morris couple murder, they would hang him.

Ruthless Operation

Floyd Smith cried out in despair that he knew nothing of the Morris murder. The men proceeded to tighten the rope and haul him into the air by his neck. Again, they demanded he confess.

After letting him struggle in the air for some time, they lowered him down, and gasping for breath, he again insisted on his innocence. Moments later, they loaded him into another sleigh. In the process, his blindfold slipped, enabling him to see his surroundings. He recognized a specific livery team from Decatur. He was certain of this, as he had formerly owned one of the horses.

Loading him roughly into this new sleigh, they drove on a short distance, only to stop again. Once again, they asked him to confess. This time they demanded he tell them that on the night of the murder he drove James Matteson (the brother of Milo Matteson) to the Morris house. He proclaimed that he did not know James Matteson, and they again dragged him from the sleigh and repeated the hanging operations.

After letting him down a second time, with him still professing his innocence, they again loaded him into the sleigh and drove on. His abductors stopped two more times, each time repeating the hanging operation and each time letting him back down after he dangled by his neck until he lost his senses. Each time he struggled to breathe, and the world spun around him.

Each of these operations was accompanied by kicks and blows, bruising him in the ribs, legs and arms. By the fourth time, he was having difficulty standing when they stood him up. This time, in addition to asking him for a confession and his again proclaiming his innocence, one voice responded, "Well, let's hang him for good this time and dig his grave."

With that, a few of the men produced shovels and began digging a hole as the others pulled him onto his feet again and hauled him up by the rope. After he regained consciousness, they asked him to confess again. Floyd told them they could kill him if they chose, but he knew nothing of the Morris affair.

One of the men then turned to the other men standing out of Floyd's view, and asked, "Are you satisfied of his innocence?" The men replied that they were.

A man then walked Floyd a short distance away from the group into the woods and removed the bandage from his eyes. He asked him if he knew his way home. Floyd said he did not. The man pointed him the way home and also told him he had saved his life. He pretended to be his friend and made Floyd solemnly promise to tell no one, not even his wife, what had been done to him that evening.

Slightly disoriented, Floyd made the painful long walk home, arriving around ten o'clock in the evening. The livery team that Floyd had identified was later noted as arriving back at the stable in Decatur around the same time.

Constable Botsford reported that the prisoner was taken from him and later rescued and told to go home. On reaching home, Floyd recovered and sent word for a journalist from the local newspaper to come to his home.

The reporter arrived, and Floyd recounted his experience that night. He stated there were five men in all who abducted him. He was able to identify three of them: the man at the end who released him and two others he saw through the slit in the blindfold. He also said he was confident he could identify the other two men by their voices, explaining he thought they were the constable and his deputy.

Denying involvement in the abduction, Constable Botsford maintained that Smith was taken from him and his deputy by armed men who claimed they were friends of Charles Morris.

OUTRAGED CITIZENRY

In the days that followed the incident with Floyd Smith, the prosecuting attorney for Van Buren County, Benjamin F. Heckert, and Sheriff Nathan Thomas, along with his deputies, were questioned about the operation, and none of them had any knowledge.

The entire event appeared to have been an invention of Constable Warren Botsford in his attempt to solve the crime by drawing a connection between Milo Matteson and the Morris murders, either through a witness connecting his brother James to the scene or some other hitman.

Botsford continued to deny any knowledge or involvement with the evening abduction of Floyd Smith. When the story was released to the newspapers in the following days, the alleged violation to humanity and decency sparked outrage all over the region. Citizens demanded the matter be investigated by the county.

Despite the outrage over the incident with Floyd Smith in December, as the New Year approached, members of the community still had uppermost in their minds that the Matteson-Morris forgery case had something to do with the murders. Milo Matteson was considered by many to be a money shark, and now that he was living in Chicago, suspicions continued to brew. Considering that the killer had driven to and abandoned the Morris horse in South Bend and likely had taken a train to the Windy City, theories abounded that this linked to Matteson.

It was believed by many who had followed the Matteson-Morris case that had Charles Morris lived, when the U.S. District Court ruled in his favor, he would have likely pressed criminal charges against Matteson for the forgery. It was suspected Matteson knew this would be the outcome, as he could not prove the money was ever given to Morris.

With this, Matteson was indeed facing prison time once this inevitable outcome was reached. Now with Charles Morris and his wife suddenly out of the way, he settled quickly with the Morris family members on the estate to hasten his departure from Michigan.

Following the murders, members of the press recollected an earlier murder that many considered may have had a connection to the Matteson-Morris case. Marshall Simpson Pritchard, a friend of Charles Morris, whose wife was originally from the Prairie Ronde area, claimed that he was in possession of facts that would make him a valuable witness in the mortgage case before the U.S. District Court. Pritchard was found murdered with a single gunshot to the head near Rockford, Illinois, on Friday, January 24, 1879.

The scene was staged to appear to be suicide, with a gun placed nearby. The killer made an error, however, and placed it near the wrong hand. The thirty-four-year-old Pritchard worked as a tax collector for the township of Cherry Valley and for some time prior to his death had reported to friends he believed he was being shadowed through the day and followed home.

Pritchard's body was found lying on a small pile of straw early in the morning at the side of a roadway on North Main Street (Mill Street today), not far from Cherry Valley Cemetery. A man taking his cow out to its enclosure discovered him and notified the constable.

A neighbor, Sophia Sandine, who lived directly across from where he was found, reported being woken in the middle of the night by the sounds of two male voices talking. A short time later, she heard a pistol shot around eleven o'clock and afterward heard a team of horses pulling a sleigh riding away. As it was late at night, she was too afraid to go out to investigate.

Pritchard was found with $100 in a pocketbook in the coat pocket that lay underneath him, and another pocket had been turned out with coin found scattered on the ground. A clump of hair had been pulled out of his head and found on his breast, as if he had been in a fight. The pistol found next to him was about three feet away. It appeared rusty, as if the chamber had not seen shells in it for quite some time.

Pritchard's plan had been to be in Rockford and in Cherry Valley Township collecting taxes on Friday and Saturday. While in the village of Cherry Valley, he had also visited some of the saloons. Although known to drink occasionally, he was by no means known to drink to intoxication. Investigators later discovered his tax book at Mapes' Saloon but were uncertain if he had left it there or someone else had placed it there.

It was theorized that Pritchard had been induced to leave the saloon by a "festive" companion for the purpose of visiting someone else in the direction of the cemetery. While walking in that direction, Pritchard perhaps sensed he was being set up and objected to going any further, whereupon a fight broke out and he was shot. After the killer hastily searched Pritchard pockets, the assailant's companion rode up in the sleigh and the two rode away, but not before attempting to stage the scene as a suicide. Pritchard left behind a wife and an eight-year-old son.

As the public brewed over the mystery of the Morris murders, the feverish state of public sentiment was rising when the press refreshed their memory of this earlier tragedy. Many in Rockford and the Cherry Valley area believed Pritchard had been assassinated. Had Matteson been involved with the death of Pritchard? Or was this merely a botched robbery attempt on a tax collector that turned lethal?

Ugly stories also circulated about James Matteson, the brother of Milo, who was a known "outlaw" and "desperate character." It was learned that he, too, had left Michigan and returned to Texas right after the Morris murders.

Smith Arrested Again

A few days after the first incident, Floyd Smith was rearrested and brought into Decatur by Constable Botsford for questioning before the magistrate. During the examination, Smith relayed his experiences about the night he alleged he was abducted.

Following this, Constable Botsford was called to the stand. He testified that the reason he had arrested Floyd Smith was that Smith had told him Matteson had come to him the day after the murder of Morris.

Botsford claimed Matteson had told Smith that they would detain his mail at the post office, and to avoid that, he was having his mail be addressed to Smith's house. Matteson had explained that his mail would come addressed to Smith and would have a special mark on one corner of the envelope to distinguish it. He allegedly had asked Smith to set this mail aside and he would send someone to come pick it up. The mail continued to arrive that way until Smith's wife became suspicious when Matteson's mail was being turned over to someone else.

Floyd Smith was charged with complicity in the murder of Charles and Esther Morris. The trial was delayed twice and finally commenced on January 15, 1880. With a short session, the trial was adjourned, and Floyd Smith was discharged for the want of testimony that would bind him over to the court. In essence, there was not sufficient evidence to support the charge of his involvement in the murder, and the judge released him.

Conclusion

Despite attempts at following up on leads, the prosecution's efforts to build a case against Floyd Smith never materialized. They were not able to assemble witnesses to support charges of his involvement in the case. No further direct evidence, beyond community suspicion, ever connected Matteson directly with the murders.

In terms of evidence, the gun used in the Morris murders was originally believed to be either a Remington revolver or a navy Colt. The bullets found at the scene were determined to have come from the same gun. Eventually, a few of the bullets were taken to Chicago for examination by dealers and gunsmiths. All of the experts concluded that the size and shape of the rounds implied they could not have come from a gun manufactured in the United States. Despite this, and many other clues, none definitively pointed toward any one suspect.

As time rolled on, no one else was ever charged in the Morris murder case. The case remains unsolved.

Did Matteson arrange the assassination? Was Floyd Smith involved, or was he innocent as he proclaimed? Was there something to the South Bend connection with Riley Huntley? Or was it someone else that remained undetected?

Aside from Matteson, who else benefited from the deaths of Charles and Esther Morris? One could speculate his brothers who inherited the farm could be placed on that list. Is it possible resentment existed among his siblings over Charles inheriting the family homestead? If so, why was Esther shot so many more times than Charles?

Throughout the many decades, historians have explored this case. Some have suggested Esther was pregnant at the time of her death with a lover's child. However, this is likely conjecture, as no records seem to exist indicating an autopsy was performed to support this.

It also appears that Jennie Bull was never considered a suspect. She was the last person to have seen them alive. Could it be she was involved? Could she really have slept through the night with so many gunshots downstairs? With her room right upstairs, it does lead one to wonder why she was dismissed as a suspect.

Perhaps the key to unraveling the mystery around this murder is not asking why Charles was murdered, but more so, why was Esther? The killer assassinated Charles outside. He could have easily made his escape in the chaos, giving him time to still make it to the barn and escape. Instead, he continued inside to kill Esther. If we suppose he killed Esther to avoid leaving witnesses or feared she might identify him before he could steal the horse, why did he not kill Jennie? If he was indeed familiar with the home, how could he have overlooked her being upstairs? Why risk leaving a potential

Morris marker at Anderson Cemetery, Lawton, Michigan. *Author collection.*

witness? Did he not know she was home? Or could she have been in on the murders?

When you mull through the details of this case, it presents so many unanswered questions. The Morris murders case has not been forgotten in Van Buren or Cass Counties, and it remains a part of local folklore.

The funeral for Charles and Esther Morris took place at their home on Tuesday, September 30, 1879, at two o'clock. About two thousand people from the community attended. The couple was interred at Anderson Cemetery in Lawton, about half a mile from their home along an unpaved road. The cemetery was once on their own farm, and they were laid to rest beside their only child, who had died the previous winter.

The *Time Herald* wrote on October 3, 1879, about their burial beside their child: "How sudden and how terrible is the summons that calls them to slumber by its side in the wild and lonely burial place near by their deserted household."

Today, the words "Murdered at their own home on the night of September 28, 1879," are etched into their headstone, still calling for answers a century and a half later.

5

DOWN THE VINTNER'S WELL

(1887)

For a time the story was accepted, but gradually the suspicions of the neighbors had been growing that all was not right and the matter culminated early this morning in half a dozen of the neighbors digging out the well that had been filled in.

—Battle Creek Daily Journal, *August 8, 1888*

In the mid-1800s, Charles Chidester, a vintner and farmer in Convis Township, Calhoun County, developed seedlings from the Concord seed for a new variety of grapes known as the Chidester Grape, which grew in three different types numbered 1, 2 and 3. Depending on the variety, the grape was either purple or a brownish-purple and grew in clusters resembling a Concord, only smaller and of good quality, and all three had the characteristics of a strong vine. The first variety fruit ripened one week earlier than the New England Moore's Early, the second was known for its size and hardiness similar to a Concord and the third could endure well until January without dropping berries. The grapes were of the *Vitis labrusca* species, the largest number of cultivated varieties known for being hardy and productive, with fibrous roots, heavy branching and abundant.

Chidester grapes. *From* Our Native Grape, *C. Mitzky and Co., 1893.*

MORNING EXCAVATION

On August 14, 1888, Charles Chidester enlisted the help of neighbors to help him dig out a well on his property that had been filled in for a full year. A half-dozen neighbors offered to help in the task, and they began excavating the well just after sunrise. The men took turns digging, using hand shovels as the hole became deeper with their work. The clink of shovels striking against the occasional stone echoed across the vineyard and nearby pastures covered in morning dew.

Around nine o'clock that morning, Frank Cooley and James McHale, two of the younger volunteers, were digging down in the hole, now about six feet deep, when they made a disturbing find. In the sublayer of muddy soil, just as they reached the water table, a partially decomposed corpse of a man was uncovered in the mud. The man was lying sideways with his head angled downward.

Moments after the grisly find, Chidester returned to the excavation to check on progress. The stunned men reported their discovery to him, directing Chidester to look into the pit they had dug. He ordered them to desist further work, giving instructions for Frank and James to ride into Battle Creek and notify Deputy Sheriff Alden Powell. After being alerted, the deputy in turn contacted Alexander Briggs, the county coroner.

As the four men were returning to the farm, Coroner Briggs instructed them to pick up Dr. Wirt Lamoreaux on the way. Upon their arrival on the scene around ten o'clock, after ordering the corpse carefully exhumed from the well, the doctor examined the body.

Dr. Lamoreaux determined that the skull had been fractured by a blunt instrument and the blow was sufficient to have caused death. He noted it

Chidester farm, 1873 Atlas. *Willard Library Archives.*

was impossible to determine if any other blows had been dealt to the rest of the body, as it was in a high state of decomposition. The feet and hands had entirely rotted off, and the skin on the scalp was sloughed off in decay. It had been lying in wet soil for an estimated twelve months.

Later, a more detailed examination of the body at his office would indicate that the injuries to the skull had been likely caused by three distinct blows from a hammer. Two of the blows were close together over the left ear, and the third, much more severe, had left a round hole driven cleanly through the back of the skull.

The Missing Man

The body was identified by the remains of clothing and determined to be that of George Campbell, a twenty-five-year-old man who disappeared in the vicinity around August 1887. George supposedly sent word that he was headed out west. As this journey was something he had spoken of in the past, for a time the story was accepted.

Gradually, however, the neighbors' suspicions grew. His abrupt departure without bidding goodbye was not Campbell's nature. Something was not quite right about his leaving. With the discovery of his body at the bottom of a filled-in well, their dark suspicions became suddenly verified. Campbell had been murdered.

In one of his pockets, they found the sum of six or seven dollars in silver. The body lay on its side across the length of the well and appeared to have been laid there, rather than thrown in from above. He was buried about six feet from the surface, and there was nothing found in the well that he could have broken his skull on, affirming this was no accident.

Frank House

With very little investigation, the path in the search for Campbell's killer led the deputy straight to a thirty-year-old man named Frank House. Frank was the man who was now in possession of Campbell's property, having reported to the victim's family that he had purchased the land, a pair of horses, harnesses and a wagon and a plough from him before George supposedly headed west. Frank had presented a bill of sale to George Campbell's mother, relaying the news of his sudden departure, and she had believed him.

House had been working and living at the Campbell farm since that time. Other neighbors reported to have seen him wearing a wristwatch that had previously been worn by Campbell, as well as carrying a revolver once owned by the man.

Coroner Briggs decided that with the strong evidence against House, who happened to be present when the body was removed, House was to be placed under arrest. Deputy Sheriff Powell escorted him to the Marshall, Michigan jail later that evening, charging him with murder. Frank House maintained his innocence, and there were some who believed him, as he had participated in the excavation of the well with the other men. The general consideration was: if he had known what they would find, why did he not run away?

That same morning, Esther Austin, Campbell's mother, had arrived in town. She was accompanied by her daughter, the victim's sixteen-year-old half-sister. She had not yet been contacted about the discovery. It was only when she had stopped by to see her son-in-law Frank Cooley, some three miles from her home, that she was informed.

On hearing the news, her daughter advised her to ride into town to call on Judge Tolman Hall, to enquire about legal matters that might be precipitated by the discovery. Esther Austin made a statement in the presence of the judge, going on record with an official complaint against Frank House and charging him with the murder of her son.

She was aware of the rumors circulating in the preceding months about Frank House—up to that point she had dismissed them. She recalled how she had spoken with her son before his departure on the evening of August 4, 1887, when he was last seen. He had asked her, "What would you say if I went away, without milking the cows?" indicating his desire to move west. She had told him that it would be OK. Later, he had said laughingly to his sister when he left that evening, "You may never see me again."

After that he had gone over to Chidester's farm, where he was in the habit of spending his evenings. That was the last Esther or her daughter had seen George. She said it was later reported to her that he had left the Chidester farm around ten o'clock that evening and was last observed standing on the road talking to Frank House. No one had reported seeing him since.

A few days later, she received a letter at the Bellevue Post Office dated August 8. The letter writer purported to be a friend of her son and said that George had hurt his hand, so he had dictated the letter. The letter requested she not be so attached to the team of horses he had sold to Frank House, along with the land, and asserted that Frank would pay her the money due George to her. She had handed the letter to Frank House, and he had read it. She did not know what happened to the letter after that, but believed Frank had destroyed it, though she was not certain.

In addition to the team of horses and other articles mentioned, House claimed to have purchased half interest in the existing corn crop on the land. Esther Austin had heard her son say he was considering selling his land and team of horses to House, but it was unclear to her whether he had actually received the money for it. Any sales information she received had come directly from Frank House after her son supposedly headed west.

What the citizens of Calhoun County did not know about Frank House was that he had served a year in the state prison in Jackson for forgery following a conviction on May 6, 1881, in Macomb County.

Suspicions

Many months went by from the time Esther Austin had received that letter. There was no further word from George. The following year, as the summer wore on, neighbors began to suggest to her that she should make a complaint against Frank House to the authorities. They began to suspect House knew more about George's disappearance than he was letting on, and many believed he harbored a dark secret.

Neighbors began to speculate that Frank House had killed and buried George Campbell somewhere. A likely location was in Chidester's well, which had been discovered to have been mysteriously filled in the previous fall, to the surprise of the aging vintner. They did not believe that George would leave without others knowing about the terms of his agreement, and he certainly would not have sent a letter to do so. It was these rumors and suspicions that motivated Charles Chidester to have the well excavated that August morning.

While in custody at the Marshall jail, Frank House showed no signs of agitation or concern, which some believed was an indication of his innocence. He did later complain, however, about the conditions at the jail, stating there were bedbugs and the food was terrible. Eventually, when the judge read him the charges, he evinced trembling hands and a slight quiver of the lips. Prior to that, he had acquiesced willingly when he was incarcerated.

While in custody, further suspicion made his story begin to appear to be far and wide from the truth. He told the sheriff he had placed the letter allegedly written by Campbell in a curry box tin in Esther Austin's barn, but when the barn was searched, it was not found. Statements regarding his interactions with Campbell, and his own movements on the night the man went missing, did not align with other witness accounts.

Inquest

The formal inquest conducted by Coroner Briggs moved to a formal hearing before a jury beginning on August 21. Edward Austin, a half-brother of George Campbell, was the first witness called to testify.

Edward had seen George at his mother's house at dinner the night he had disappeared. He described what George had been wearing, which matched the clothes his body was found in. He also said his brother had not told him goodbye when he left that evening, nor did he say anything about going away west.

Esther Austin also testified to seeing George at dinner that evening. She gave the same description of the clothes he was last seen wearing, and although she did confirm that George had frequently spoken of going west, the last time she had heard him speak of it, he had indicated his intentions were to do so after the threshing was done on the present harvest, which was months away. In her mind, George was expected to return that evening, but he had not.

Esther Austin also recounted that George had mentioned he intended to sell his team and harness to Frank House a few weeks before he left. Later, Frank had approached her and asked her if she was willing to sell the team, and she had referred him to George. She never heard if an arrangement had been made, but she knew George had paid $240 for the team earlier in the spring.

After George disappeared, Frank approached her to ask if he could keep the team he had purchased from George in the same barn, and she agreed, as long as he would take care of cleaning and feeding them. Frank came every day to clean out their stalls and feed them the oats left for them by George.

She further testified that George had told her two weeks before he left that he had sold his plow, wristwatch and revolver to Frank House but never mentioned anything else. It was House who had told her that he had given George money for half of the corn as well. She had no way to verify whether this was true.

Esther recalled the day she had last seen George, he had mentioned that he might go over to Ceresco to visit a doctor he knew over there but had not said anything about leaving to head west.

James Wood, another neighbor, testified to having spoken with Frank House about George Campbell. He asked him if he had taken George to Battle Creek the night he left. House had replied, "No, I had taken him to the train station." He also told him he had paid $250 to George for the team.

Another neighbor, James McHale, explained that he had seen George on the night he was last seen, sitting in front of the barn at Chidester's. George had asked James to join a baseball club meeting later that evening, and initially he told George he was in a hurry. However, a few minutes later, after thinking it over, he asked George what time the meeting was. It was then that he observed George looking at his watch, checking the time. He remembered it as being a silver watch, similar to the one found with Frank House.

A jeweler from Bellevue, Fran Avery, would later confirm that the watch found in the possession of Frank House was the one formerly owned by George Campbell. Many other witnesses testified to having seen House with the watch in his possession following the disappearance of Campbell.

The account of events given by Frank House, when compared with the testimony of Esther Austin, added to the suspicion that he had committed the crime. On October 17, another story emerged of an incident that happened three years prior. It seems a man by the name of James Evans from Pennfield had ridden his wagon into Battle Creek with a load of wheat in the company of Frank House. After selling the wheat, he had put his team of horses in the barn at a livery stable in the city. In addition to selling the wheat, he had also collected $50 for the sale of two cows, making over $100, which he had on his person.

Evans was last seen going to a restaurant with Frank House in Battle Creek for dinner, and he was never seen again. He did not return home and was never heard from again. A search was made for him by friends, but no cause for his disappearance was ever uncovered. He left behind a wife and three small children. After the unearthing of George Campbell, neighbors in the area began to suspect that James Evans may have met a similar fate.

Deputy Sheriff Powell investigated these claims that House was somehow involved in the disappearance of Evans but discovered that House was in the Dakota Territory delivering some horses for a man, having left on March 30, 1885. Evans had disappeared on April 16, and it was positively proven that House was still out of state during that time. The witness accounts of seeing House together with the missing man were soon dismissed as misidentification.

The sentencing of Frank House. *From the* Marshall Statesman, *December 21, 1888.*

During the coroner's inquiry, Frank House admitted to filling the well. He had worked for Chidester and claimed he told his employer the well was dry. He said he filled it in after asking Chidester if he should, indicating that the hogs were running free in the nearby orchard and might be at risk of falling in.

Chidester denied ever telling House to fill the well in, nor having any conversation about the hogs. Witnesses who had excavated the body testified that no one could have filled that well in without noticing the body at the bottom, as it was only about six feet down to the water line. It would have been clearly visible.

The coroner's jury found Frank House guilty, especially after he admitted to having filled in the well. The jury determined that Frank House had killed Campbell with some blunt object, likely a hammer, and thrown him into the well. The official trial would not begin until December of that year.

The Trial

Over eighty witnesses were subpoenaed to appear, and the intensity of public interest was at its peak when the trial began on December 10, 1888. The jury was selected by the close of the second day, chosen from all over the county. They were sequestered in the Tremont House in Marshall during the proceedings.

The trial lasted until Saturday, December 15, when both the prosecution and defense finally rested their cases. The jury went into deliberation that afternoon. After being gone only two hours, they returned with a verdict of murder in the first degree. The judge, having confirmed the verdict by roll call of the jury, delivered the sentence of life imprisonment.

Frank House, when reality struck that he was returning to prison, turned pale as the sentence was given to him. He declined any supper following his last day in court and was taken by train the following morning to the Michigan State Prison in Jackson. He arrived on December 16, 1888, and died in the prison hospital on January 20, 1893.

6
MORNING OF BLOOD AND MIRACLES

(1889)

What could have caused this most horrible butchery is a mystery. Speculation, which covers the widest possible scope, has developed but one theory in regard to it, and that is the fact that Westbrook, through bad business judgement or poor management a few months ago, had met with financial losses. These, it is supposed, preyed upon his mind until reason was dethroned.
—Weekly Expositor, *November 14, 1889*

Haggai Wesbrook was born in Ontario, Canada. His Canadian-born parents were Mordecai and Mary Anne (Shaver) Wesbrook. He was raised on a farm and became a stockman and a farmer, learning animal husbandry and crop cultivation from his father.

A Troubled Father

In February 1849, Haggai Wesbrook married an English woman, Emily Scott, in Canada. Their first five children were born in Ontario, and then in 1860 the Wesbrooks relocated to Vergennes Township, Kent County, Michigan.

During his immigration to the United States, the family name Wesbook was changed to Westbrook on all of their naturalization documents. Haggai and Emily went on to have two more children after their arrival in Michigan.

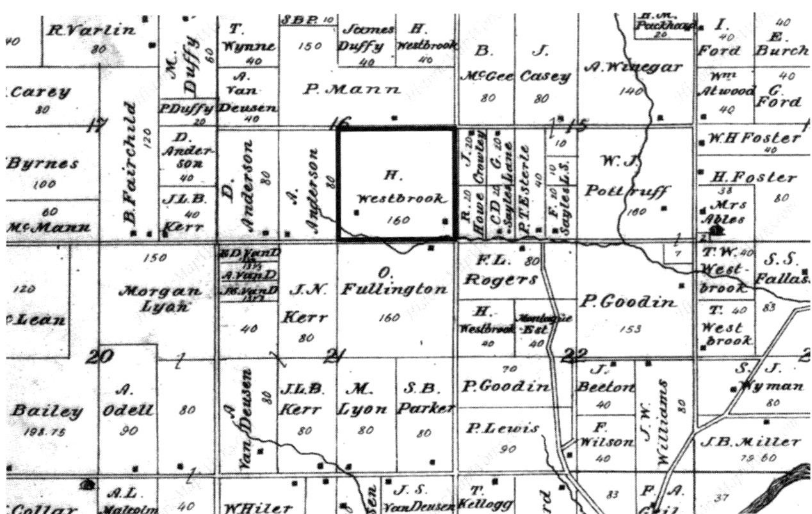

Westbrook farm, Vergennes Township, Kent County Atlas, 1876. *Library of Congress.*

Sadly, four of their children died young, two in infancy. Their three surviving children were Charles, Mary and James.

Emily Westbrook passed away in 1871.

In 1872, Haggai married Melissa Snow, the daughter of Uriah Snow from Sparta, Michigan. Together they would have five children: Frederic, Laura, Rhoda, Ira and Alice. In Vergennes Township, Haggai was regarded as an industrious farmer. He was a deeply religious man who took an active role in the Free Methodist Church.

By 1889, he was just over sixty years old, and his three children from his first marriage had since moved out and on with their lives away from the family farm. His youngest son with his first wife, Emily, James Henry Westbrook, had gone into the seminary and became a Methodist minister.

In 1888, Haggai had been somewhat unfortunate in his business and began to become mired in debt, which hampered the production on his farm. Friends in the community came to his aid and helped him secure a loan to pay his pressing debts. The result was that his 160-acre farm along with another 40-acre wooded parcel he owned, was encumbered with a mortgage of $3,000, which was unsettling to Haggai. In time, the holders of the mortgage began to demand payments, and though he was a hardworking man, he was not able to make much headway with managing, much less settling the debt.

With the increased pressure from the mortgage holders, Haggai was progressively unable to sleep at night. For some time, his children had witnessed him frequently falling asleep in his seat while riding in his buggy, and they often surveilled him when he went out to make sure he did not hurt himself by nodding off when traveling.

Despite this, none of his friends or family relations ever thought Haggai more than just discouraged, albeit exhausted from his labors. Most assumed he would just work through his situation with industry. That would all change in the autumn of that year.

MORNING OF MADNESS

Early in the morning of Monday, November 4, 1889, Haggai rose around four o'clock, while his wife and children were still sleeping in their beds. He dressed in his work clothes. Neglecting to put on his boots, barefooted he went to the kitchen. An autumn chill was in the air. It had been another restless night.

Haggai had often used a carpenter's hammer when he needed to terminate sheep and cattle on his farm. Carrying an oil lamp in one hand and the hammer he had procured from a shelf in the kitchen in the other, he returned to the bedroom where his wife, Melissa, slept. Pausing only for a moment in the flicker of the lamplight, he struck her with three heavy blows to the forehead, fracturing her skull. Melissa made no sound.

Leaving her unconscious, he went to the bedroom where three of his daughters—Laura (fourteen), Rhoda (twelve) and Alice (fifteen months)—slept. Haggai, still carrying the lamp, swiftly dealt all three of the daughters similar blows to their heads. Subtle moans from his victims broke through the morning silence on the ground floor.

Haggai then crept quietly upstairs to the room where his two sons Ira (eight) and Frederic (sixteen) slept. Frederic was sleeping on his side with his face against the wall. Haggai approached the teen's bedside, setting the lamp down on a dresser, before striking his first blow. Perhaps he had begun to lose his nerve, or maybe it was the just the angle of his son's repose in the lamplight, but his swing resulted only in a glancing blow off the boy's forehead.

Suddenly awakened by the jolt, Frederic jumped out of bed onto his feet. Slightly stunned but filled with adrenaline, the young man was able to react before the second blow came. Catching the weapon with both his hands, he cried out, "Why, Pa! What are you doing?" while he wrenched the hammer from his father's fingers.

Having lost the hammer, Haggai turned in a panic, ran out of the room and fled down the stairs. Frederic fell back on the floor, momentarily stunned from what just happened, and then pulled on his pants and followed in pursuit of his father. When the boy passed his mother's room, he heard her moaning and entered to discover she had also been attacked.

Haggai had disappeared somewhere out of the house, and Frederic rushed out of the front door to ring the farm bell to alert the neighbors. The clanging sound echoed over the fields in the dark before sunrise, a universal alarm across the morning fog.

In turning toward the kitchen door from ringing the bell, Frederic discovered the body of his father stretched on the ground nearby in a pool of blood, deceased.

Dawn of Carnage

The neighbors were aroused but arrived at the scene slowly. Those who did appear witnessed a scene of carnage in the predawn hours. Melissa lay moaning with blood and wounds on her forehead, bloody hands clutching her face bewildered and in pain. The three daughters were equally covered in crimson, and the body of Haggai barefoot lay prostrate on the ground outside the home with his throat cut.

When the immediate situation was assessed after Frederic briefed the arriving neighbors, a messenger was sent to nearby Lowell, a journey of six miles, in search of a doctor and medical aid, as well as to notify the authorities.

Dr. McDonnell from Lowell was the first to arrive. He examined Melissa Westbrook and believed there would be a chance of recovery. He then examined the three daughters, and although they were still alive, he initially did not have a lot of certainty whether they would recover.

Laura's injuries appeared the most severe, followed by baby Alice. Rhoda's injuries appeared to be three glancing blows, but she was bleeding outwardly. All three girls were swollen and comatose by the time the doctor arrived.

Haggai Wesbrook, failing to kill his son, had slashed his own throat three times with a razor, eventually cutting a carotid artery, from which he bled out. He died almost instantly. Frederic was eventually examined, and the first blow to his head had resulted in only a bruise.

It was considered by many that only a miracle saved him. Ira, the younger boy, awoke to hearing the sounds of his mother and sisters downstairs and the clangor of bells. He was found safe hiding under the covers in his bed clothes when neighbors stormed the home.

RUMORS AND FABRICATIONS

Justice John L. Covert arrived at the scene as the day wore on and impaneled a coroner's jury to hold an inquest the following day. The determination of the jury was that Haggai Westbrook had gone insane, attacked his family and took his own life. Newspapers across the state soon ran with the story of the insane farmer who "murdered his whole family." A funeral for Haggai Westbrook was held the following day, and he was buried at Bailey Cemetery in Lowell Township.

It was clear that Melissa Westbrook, although severely injured with skull fractures, would make a full recovery. However, what shocked even the medical doctor was when the baby, Alice, regained consciousness late the following day. Despite having three frightening-looking marks on her head, she soon was smiling and manifesting a desire to play as if nothing had happened.

On Wednesday, Laura and Rhoda were also awake, although vomiting and miserable. The two girls' road to recovery was tentative at best. Their faces and heads were blue and swollen, and both had severe concussions. The injuries received that morning would plague them in various ways throughout their lives, but as if by a miracle, they, too, survived.

MIRACLE OF SURVIVAL

Facts on the true condition of the family were slow to propagate to the press. The horrible scene on discovery of apparently lifeless bodies led to erroneous reports being telegrammed to newspapers across the state that all the victims were dead. For several weeks after this tragedy, newspapers, whether embellishing or just running to press with misinformation, circulated the news across the country that the entire family had died, save one son. "Murder-Suicide," "Horrible Homicide" and "Horrid Butchery" were just a few shocking headlines that dominated the papers.

Headstone of Haggai Wesbrook. Bailey Cemetery, Lowell, Michigan. *Findagrave.com.*

By November 22, the headlines and stories had begun to catch up with reality. New updated reports relayed that Haggai Westbrook had, in fact, attempted to murder his family, but they all were recovering or at least were expected to recover. In fact, all of the children would survive and live until adulthood, and the only one to die that day was their father, Haggai Westbrook.

Their mother, Melissa, would recover and live to the age of seventy-eight, passing away in 1930. Laura would live to age eighty-seven, passing away in 1963. Rhoda would struggle with the effects of that night and live until age forty-two, passing away in 1920. Alice would go on to marry and have three sons but struggled the last twenty years of her life with increasing illnesses, and passed away in 1956 at the age of sixty-seven.

Frederic passing away in 1944, lived to the age of seventy-one. His younger brother, Ira, died in an automobile accident on Labor Day weekend 1962 at the age of eighty-one.

What drove Haggai Westbrook to assault his family? Was it a willful act or a moment of insanity brought about by severe stress, as was reported? Or could it have been something no one seemed to consider at the time, such as a case of homicidal somnambulism, also known as sleepwalking? Today the National Library of Medicine lists cases that have used homicidal somnambulism as a legal defense, which has led to acquittal in some trials.

Haggai Westbrook was found without his shoes, something the family noted he was never known to do. Was this his intent to creep silently, or was this an indicator of a sleep-deprived man in a dissociative state who acted out violence while sleeping? Or was it really just reason, dethroned?

7

THE PENSIONER'S MONEY

(1892)

One of the cruelest, most inhuman and atrocious murders ever chronicled was that which came to light at Grand Ledge on Wednesday.
—Lansing State Journal, *November 18, 1892*

In 1890, Congress passed the Dependent Pension Act, which granted men with a disability who served in the Union Army a pension of $8 a month, whether or not their condition was service-related, provided they had served over ninety days during the Civil War. Incidentally, this act also granted pensions to their widows and heirs based on the veteran's service, with an additional $2 for each child under sixteen years of age in their household.

The Pensioner

In 1892, William Lampman was a pensioner who was seventy-five years old, and he lived in his own home in Grand Ledge, Michigan. He had served in Company F, in the Twenty-First Michigan Infantry, which saw action in the Battles of Perryville, Stones River, Chickamauga and many others.

He was described as an elderly white-haired gentleman and a good citizen who lived inoffensively, although somewhat miserly. William moved to Grand Ledge in 1886 from Stanton, Michigan, and often boasted that it only cost him sixty cents a week to live, his regular diet being bread, milk and halibut.

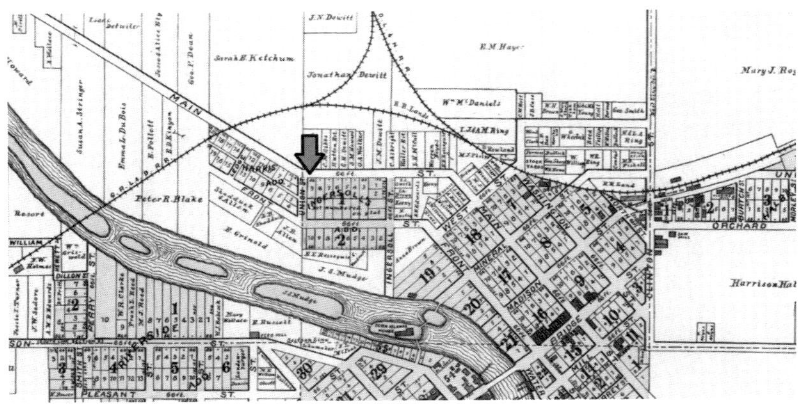

Where Lampman lived. *1895 Eaton County Map. Bullock, Taggart and Morrell.*

He was known in the community as "Uncle Billy" and had built an addition on the front of his home, renting it out for additional income.

The house was a one-story dwelling, situated on the corner of Main and Union Streets, about a quarter mile from the train depot for the Grand Rapids, Lansing & Detroit Railway. The front of the house addition consisted of a bedroom and two closets, and the rear of the building was a lean-to with a kitchen and a small bedroom where William resided. The only furniture in William's bedroom was a bed, a chair and a dresser bureau.

William had lived in that small room alone since his wife died. He usually cleaned his own room and cooked his meals in the kitchen. Occasionally, he would take meals at the home of a neighbor named Wallace. He lived simply and was friendly with those he interacted with in the community.

William's pension was not tremendous, but it allowed him to live comfortably in the back room of his house. Within a few years of receiving his pension, William managed to save a little over $400, mostly from back pension money owed to him, which he normally kept in a bank. He had also sold a city lot the previous fall for a small amount of money. In early November, however, he had withdrawn about $300 of his money from the bank and was rumored to have kept it hidden in his room.

William rented the room in the front part of his house to Frank Butcher, his wife and child. On Sunday, November 13, the Butcher family left town for a few days to visit relatives in Eagle and Belding.

In their absence, they had made arrangements for William to walk next door to a neighbor's house and take his meals with them until they returned. Although William often prepared his own food, Mrs. Butcher wanted to make sure he had company. She had become fond of the old pensioner and worried he might be lonely in their absence.

On Monday, November 14, William ate breakfast with the neighbors as scheduled. By the time of the noonday meal, referred to as dinner during this era, William was absent. The neighbors did not think much of his missing this meal, assuming William had decided to stay home and eat alone. When he did not arrive in the evening, they again assumed he had made other arrangements and did not think to check up on him.

Discovery

Mrs. Butcher returned on Wednesday to Grand Ledge for her baby carriage. When she arrived at the train station, she asked a man going near her home to kindly bring the carriage over to her in town. Arriving at the home, the man discovered the front door was wide open. Thinking something was wrong, he did not enter and instead brought the news to Mrs. Butcher.

She hastened home, concerned for her landlord, and also found the front door open. She entered and discovered the door to William's room was ajar. Being afraid to enter, she at once returned by train to Eagle, where her husband was staying, and relayed the news to him. Frank traveled home shortly after and went into William's room.

There he found the veteran deceased, lying on the floor, with wounds to his head in a graphic scene of carnage. Frank immediately notified Marshal Thomas J. Toaz, who in turn rushed to Lampman's home.

The coroner was summoned, and he took charge of the body and impaneled a jury to investigate. Many theories began to circulate, as the village of Grand Ledge was aroused when the news spread. The prevailing belief was that Lampman was murdered by persons who forcibly entered the home intent on robbery.

Marshal Toaz

Marshal Toaz was a well-respected officer in the Grand Ledge area who lived at this time in Portland. He arrived on scene and later described the experience to the *Lansing State Journal* as follows:

> *I found the old man lying on his back on the floor, with his head under the first round of the chair which stood at the head of the bed. The bureau stood opposite the bed and the space between was just large enough to allow a man's body to lie at a straight angle. His hands were crossed upon his breast and tightly bound with a hame strap, so much so that he could not have moved them. Over his face a small piece of rag carpet had been thrown. The bed clothes had been pulled off the bed and thrown back in a heap, and under them was found a green hickory club, about two feet long and two inches through, the end of which was covered in blood, doubtless the death instrument. Round his neck was tied a pair of overalls, so tightly that it was impossible to force your fingers between them and the throat. Blood was on the bed clothes and pillows and also where his head lay. He wore two pairs of overalls, the pockets of which had been searched, as had also the top drawer of the bureau. A leathern pocketbook, which he always carried, and a bunch of pension papers were gone.*

The "hame strap" described was a piece of horse tack consisting of a narrow belt of leather used to hold the two ends of a harness together with a buckle.

William Lampman's remains were taken to Undertaker Hall's rooms after being viewed by a coroner's jury. The skull was found to be crushed, likely from the first blow, which was determined to have landed just behind his right ear. The back of his right hand was badly bruised, concluded to be from his attempts to defend himself from the blows of his assailant. It was speculated there may have been more than one attacker who broke into his room on Monday evening, rousing him from his sleep.

Sheriff Samuel Pollock

Sheriff Samuel Pollock of Eaton County was also notified when the discovery was made, and he initiated an inquest into the murder in coordination with Marshal Toaz.

A Civil War veteran himself, Pollock served in the Sixth Michigan Infantry as a sergeant. During the war, following the Battle of Baton Rouge, he was noted for having dispatched the commanding officer of the Rebel forces near a sugar plantation in Louisiana, capturing his sword. Following this event, he rode to New Orleans and returned with arms and ammunition for the 110 former slaves from the plantation.

As a result of his actions, he was summoned to a meeting by his commanding officer. Samuel was expecting to be upbraided for having armed the formerly enslaved, but to his surprise, his commander commended him, and he was commissioned a major. He was then assigned as the commanding officer of the Ninety-Ninth U.S. Colored Troops in September 1863.

Pollock was captured in battle the following year during the Red River Campaign and spent six weeks in a Confederate prison camp near Cherryville. He managed to escape by constructing a raft with another prisoner, crossing the bayou. Despite men and bloodhounds following him, he was able to reach federal lines with the aid of several Black families after spending three days in the swamps.

Following this, the army moved Pollock to Key West, Florida, to recover from his ordeal. It was there that he caught yellow fever but was able to recover enough to be able to take part in the Battle of Natural Bridge, near Tallahassee, Florida. He was discharged from service following the war on April 3, 1866, after which he returned to Charlotte, Michigan.

A Man with a White Horse

As sheriff of Eaton County, he began a life of public service and found himself in charge of the investigation of the murder of William Lampman.

Sheriff Samuel Pollock. *From* The County Journal, *April 20, 2024. Rendering by Dawn Baumer.*

During the investigation, Sheriff Pollock interviewed a neighbor who stated he witnessed a white horse hitched to a road cart tied up outside Lampman's house. The neighbor gave the description of a man riding away in it, leaving the vicinity between six and seven o'clock Monday evening.

The murder was determined to have occurred before Tuesday, which made the man with the white horse the number one suspect to be identified. The investigation led Sheriff Pollock to others who described the same white horse and cart heading north on Monday evening, leading to an eventual identification of the man.

On Friday, November 18, Sheriff Pollock took the late train from Grand Ledge, going straight to Greenville, where he located his suspect at his place of residence, and placed him under arrest. The man he arrested was John Butcher, the brother of Frank Butcher.

John Butcher was described as a twenty-six-year-old common laborer, poor and unmarried. Other papers erroneously claimed he had ten children when rumors spread about his arrest. Nevertheless, the man had been identified by several people heading northwest to Greenville on the road that Monday afternoon, driving a road cart pulled by a white horse. When confronted with this information, John Butcher initially denied having any knowledge of what the sheriff was telling him.

Unheeded, Sheriff Pollock arrested John to take him back to Charlotte for questioning. In doing so, he searched his pockets and found $250 on him. When John was questioned about the source of the money, he could give no answer. During the return trip on the train with the suspect, an angry mob met the sheriff at the station in Grand Ledge, intent on lynching John Butcher. The sheriff narrowly escaped the throng with his prisoner. With firmness, Pollock transported him safely to Charlotte.

Confession and Denial

Once at the sheriff's office, John Butcher was presented with all of the evidence of the witnesses who had sighted him on the road leaving the vicinity of William Lampman. It was revealed to him that investigators had learned money was found to be missing from the home of William Lampman. Further, the Sheriff pointed out his relationship with his brother clearly gave him knowledge of the comings and goings of that household.

When challenged again on where he got the money, John Butcher confessed to having visited Lampman. He then gave a detailed account of the events that evening.

He explained that he left his family's home in Eagle and arrived in Grand Ledge. On arriving there, he bought a half pint of whiskey in a drugstore. After he had drunk most of it, he decided he wanted more.

Knowing his brother was out of town and William Lampman was going to be alone, he went over to the house, intending to ask the old man to give him some money. John admitted he rode to Grand Ledge in his cart with his white horse and visited Lampman's house after drinking the whisky. He relayed the following in his confession:

> *I thought I wanted some money, and hitched my pony and went in and asked him to give me his money. He was lying on the bed. He said no.*
>
> *I took him by the throat. He tried to yell. I took down a pair of overalls and tied them around his neck and drew them around his neck to keep him still.*
>
> *I took a pocketbook out of his pocket, and put it in my pocket, and found it contained $16.75 in bills and silver. I took the pocketbook and buried it behind the barn. After taking the money I went out and drove home, put out my horse, and went to bed. No one else was in this job with me. It does not seem possible to me that I killed the old man. I had something of a scuffle with him, and he hollered.*

Following this confession, John Butcher was charged with first-degree murder and placed in the Charlotte jail as the sheriff coordinated with the coroner and Marshal Toaz for the hearing before the magistrate.

The inquest hearing into the crime began, but almost as quickly as it started, it was adjourned on November 22, when investigators concluded that John Butcher could not have acted alone. Butcher was not willing to reveal whether he had an accomplice, and thus the hearing was delayed until December 1 to allow more time for the sheriff to investigate. Most of this delay came because it was reported that a trunk was missing from Lampman's home, an item he had previously told his daughter she was to open when he died. No trunk was found inside his room or anywhere inside the house.

John Butcher. *From the* Detroit Free Press, *March 23, 1907.*

Following his initial confession at the Charlotte jail, John Butcher, likely receiving advice from fellow inmates, remained muzzled on revealing any more information about his involvement. Investigators began to believe the crime may have been committed by two men or perhaps as many as four. At one point, as many as eight suspects were being investigated.

Sheriff Pollock was soon convinced by John's version of the events that he acted alone, although he did not admit to beating Lampman with the club. Adding strength to this conclusion, the medical doctor who completed the autopsy on William Lampman stated the cause of death was indeed strangulation and that the blows to the head were postmortem. Additionally, the leather strap found around Lampman's wrists was hypothesized to have come from the harness of John Butcher's white horse.

When this information was submitted to the court, the judge adjourned the proceedings until December 19 to review the findings. Prosecuting Attorney Horace Maynard began to assemble a case to bring to trial.

John Butcher

As a boy, John Butcher was described as peaceable. He was not known to be a troublemaker, and some even referred to his demeanor as tenderhearted. However, as an adult, he still lived under his father's roof and brooded about his condition. Never seeming to amass any great amount of money, he had been broke for quite some time.

Those who knew him claimed he spent too much time pondering how to get money without working for it, rather than just rolling up his sleeves and getting on with it. Other than his lack of industriousness, he was not reported to have a bad reputation according to Marshal Toaz, who had made inquiries about him.

Pursuit of alcohol appeared to have been the only motivation for which he came to Grand Ledge. Through the boldness of whiskey, after feeling braced up in his courage, he was able to get his hands on that coveted "wad" of cash he sought so long, even though it meant taking another life to get it. It was through the hard work of Marshal Toaz and Sheriff Pollock that his connection to the crime was discovered.

When he had been taken to jail in Charlotte, it was clear how unsophisticated he was at being a criminal. This was his first time being placed in a cell, and when John was confronted with entering the box, he turned to the sheriff and coolly remarked, "Say, I don't want to go in there. If it don't make any difference to you, I'll go back home and stay with pa."

He then pushed back on the officer to get away from the cell. Sheriff Pollock informed him sternly that he could not possibly grant his request, and with some force, into the box John Butcher went. His confession of wrapping the clothing around Lampman's neck in his own view was not an admission of guilt. Despite this opinion, it was sufficient to charge him with the crime based on the autopsy results.

The Trial

The trial held at the Circuit Court at Charlotte began in November 1892 but was delayed until the January term of the court to allow for the defense to secure the attendance of important witnesses. It did not officially continue again until April 1893, with John Butcher remaining in jail the entire time.

Once underway, the trial lasted thirteen full days, with a hard fight between the prosecution and the defense attorneys. In the final ten days of the trial, there was not even a standing place within the court, so many people came out to witness the spectacle. The *Lansing State Journal* reported on April 28:

> *Despite masterful effort by the defense counsel and the tears of tender-hearted women which were plentifully shed, the statement of Butcher was believed to be true when he confessed his connection with the crime.*

The jury returned after two and a half hours of deliberation with a verdict of guilty of murder in the first degree. The newspaper described the scene:

> *When the decision was pronounced one of the most heart-rending scenes ever enacted in the Eaton County court room was the manner in which the aged father of the doomed man gave expression of his grief.*

The presiding Judge Clement Smith delivered the first sentence to a man convicted of first-degree murder ever in his time on the bench. John Butcher was sentenced to life in the Michigan State Penitentiary in solitary confinement on April 27, 1893. When the pronouncement was made by the judge, John Butcher took his sentence as he did the verdict without the least change in his expression of indifference, a look he maintained throughout the trial and from the time of his arrest.

1903 REVIEW

In 1903, John Butcher submitted an application for commutation of his sentence and requested parole from the State Board of Pardons. His hearing was held on November 20, and his case file was reviewed, along with several letters of protest from citizens in Eaton County.

The three-man review panel made the following conclusion:

> *Butcher was tried and convicted of the murder of William Lampman. The evidence was very conclusive....*
>
> *Butcher also made a confession which was heard by several. He described fully the details of the crime, that he had used a club and a pair of big brass knuckles on the old man's head, fracturing his skull and rendering Lampman insensible. Then he tied a pair of overalls around the neck of the unconscious man and held them until he had ceased to breathe.*
>
> *We heartily agree with the hosts of citizens of Eaton County who had protested against the release of this man, and who state that the murder was a most deliberate and cold-blooded affair, and we recommend that the application be denied.*

And it was.

1907 AFFIDAVIT

In January 1907, after serving fourteen years in prison following his conviction of the murder of William Lampman, John Butcher authored an affidavit stating he was innocent and that a blacksmith named Silas Compton in Eagle, Michigan, was guilty of the crime.

The affidavit was sent to Prosecuting Attorney Elmer Peters of Eaton County. Taking the statement seriously, he issued a warrant for the arrest of Compton, who was now living in Athens, Pennsylvania.

For years, Officer Toaz had believed that another suspect was likely involved. Since the conviction of John Butcher, he was no longer marshal, but serving as constable in Portland, Michigan. His colleague in the investigation, Sheriff Pollock, had passed away following a heart attack in 1904.

In the fourteen years that John was incarcerated, Michigan had done away with the rules of solitary confinement for those serving life sentences. When Mrs. Francis O'Brien, sister of John Butcher, visited him in Jackson at the Michigan State Penitentiary, she learned the secret from John that he was supposedly withholding all of these years.

When John finally told his story to her, she consulted with attorney P.T. Colgrove of Hastings, who advised her to have John make an affidavit, which he finally did. The reason John claimed he had remained silent all of these years was due to loyalty to his brothers Frank and Morris. Together, along with Compton, the four had conceived the plan to rob Lampman, whom the quartet believed had money stashed in the house.

John stated he only intended robbery, and he only learned Lampman was murdered when he read about it in the newspapers. His affidavit would deliver a whole new insight into the probable events of the evening when William Lampman was murdered.

John Butcher's Story

John Butcher's affidavit published in the *Detroit Free Press* on March 23, 1907, detailed the following account of events:

> *My conviction was unjust. I am not guilty of the offense charged and never at any time took part in the murder of Mr. Lampman, except as I may be guilty of having taken part in a plan to take his money.*
>
> *Silas Compton, an Eagle blacksmith, with whom I came in frequent contact, informed me, as well as my brothers, that Lampman had a considerable amount of money in his possession and that it would be easy for someone to get it.*
>
> *My brother, Frank Butcher, resided in part of the house occupied by Lampman in the village of Grand Ledge. Compton had frequently visited Lampman and my brother, Frank, who lived in the front part of the house.*
>
> *A plan was agreed upon whereby my brother, Frank, was to come down the evening before and hitch his horse to the shed. The following night he was to come again and inform Lampman that he had lost some money in the straw in the shed where his horse was tied. He was to get Lampman to come out with the lantern to help him hunt for the money. While so engaged,*

Compton, my brother, Morris, and myself were to go in the house and take the money.

The plan failed. Frank and Morris decided not to enter into this plan and did not come. Compton, however, was on hand and I, John Butcher, came down with my horse and cart. Compton and myself went into Frank's room and waited for some time and finally gave up on their coming. We went into the bedroom and sat on the bed. We had liquor and took several drinks.

After some time Compton suggested we get the money alone. He suggested tying Lampman so that he could not make any noise. I told him that I would not listen to such a proposition, but he kept urging it, and finally I agreed to assist him with the understanding that he promise me that the old man was in no way to be harmed. We then went into Frank's living room and I lit his lamp. Compton suggested I go first and he would hold the lamp over my head so I could see where to go.

There we saw a jug on the floor by the pantry door that Frank had used to bring milk from home. There was a strap from an old harness to carry the jug with, and Compton set the lamp on the floor and took the strap off the jug, saying that it might come in handy. I opened the door between Frank's and Mr. Lampman's room and went into the bedroom, Compton holding the light over my head.

Robbery

He then explained that when they entered the room, Lampman was lying on the bed but not asleep. He asked what they wanted, and John tossed clothes over his head so he could not see who it was. He pulled the pocketbook out of Lampman's pocket and handed it to Compton.

Just then, they heard someone outside getting water from the well pump, and Compton told John to go outside and not let anyone come into the house. Compton placed the lamp on the bureau and was holding Lampman when John exited the room. That was the last time John claimed he was in the room.

When outside, he saw someone departing the gate, having used the well pump. They did not appear to have heard or seen anything inside the house. Shortly after, Compton came out and handed him a small package and said: "This is for you. Now, John, get your horse and go home, and never divulge a

Silas Compton. *Findagrave.com.*

word of this, for if you do, both you and your brothers and all of us will get into trouble."

Compton was standing in front of Lampman's house when John left, and that was the last he ever saw him. John reemphasized the first time he learned Lampman was dead was when he read the newspaper.

He explained that his attorney told him that his two brothers would likely be arrested as well unless he made a confession of some kind. That was how he came to make the confession he did to the sheriff, indicating he had acted alone. He did not want his brothers implicated in the crime. In this new written statement, he could no longer remember what his original confession had been.

After he was arrested, he learned that Compton had left town, leaving all of his blacksmith tools and materials behind. John said that Compton had given him about $250 that evening along with the $16.75 in the wallet, and that was the money that Marshal Toaz and Sheriff Pollock had found in his possession when he was arrested.

The officers later discovered a hidden jar he had buried in his father's barn; it contained the money he claimed was given to him by Compton.

Silas Compton

Officer Toaz had long retained the suspicion that other parties were involved in the murder of William Lampman. He was never wholly convinced that John Butcher had acted alone or that he was telling the whole story. Over the years he had continued to investigate, in hopes of discovering any other suspects.

One of the people on his list of suspects was Silas Compton. He had learned of his frequent visits to the Lampman house visiting Frank Butcher prior to the murder. When Compton had abruptly left town after John Butcher was arrested, Toaz noted this as suspicious.

Although he had no evidence that Compton was involved, he decided to keep track of him and followed his relocation to Athens, Pennsylvania. Over the years, he had periodically visited where Compton was residing and enlisted the help of another officer to monitor him. In this time, there was not a letter Compton had written or movement that he had made that Toaz was not made aware of.

In the preceding fourteen years, he had presented what evidence he had on Compton to the various prosecutors who occupied the office, but stating the case was weak, none had opted to take action. All demanded stronger evidence before taking the matter further.

When the new affidavit arrived from John Butcher, that all changed. Prosecutor Peters considered the document to be sufficient to solicit the governor of Pennsylvania, who in turn granted extradition of Compton to Michigan. Peters accompanied Officer Toaz to arrest Compton, returning him to Eaton County for prosecution in March 1907.

The Compton Trial

The trial of Silas Compton was held in June 1907 in Charlotte, Michigan. The prosecution presented evidence mostly collected by Officer Toaz, along with the affidavit from John Butcher describing his account of the murder that implicated Compton. They brought forward four witnesses who testified to seeing Compton the night the murder happened in Grand Ledge, and two were able to describe the scar on his chin.

Compton, now an older man himself, maintained his innocence. On June 26, it was the defense counsel's turn to present the case. The star witness for the defense was the former attorney for John Butcher, who testified on the stand that John had confided in him that he alone had committed the murder and had bludgeoned Lampman with the club.

The courtroom was crowded throughout the trial. Blow-by-blow accounts were watched and reported on by the press.

The Mysterious Death of Toaz

During the trial, a shocking event took place, seemingly unrelated to the Compton trial. Officer Toaz was found in his house, with all the doors locked, apparently shot in the head with his own revolver. Investigating officers adopted the theory that he took his own life, which was vehemently protested by his family and friends. They said he was a man of impeachable bravery and that if he had been mixed up in any trouble, he had the courage to face it.

Deputy Thomas J. Toaz. *From the* Detroit Free Press, *March 26, 1907. Rendering by Dawn Baumer.*

His tragic death shocked the citizens of Eaton County. Theories abounded that it was a revenge murder connected with the Compton case or perhaps another recent case where he had arrested and recently delivered to the County jail a trio of suspects accused of violating a fourteen-year-old girl.

Mrs. Toaz, who discovered her husband's body at two o'clock in the morning, had recalled hearing sounds of him struggling with someone and heard him call out, "What are you doing here?" before hearing the gunshot and everything going silent. She found him lying in the dining room with his pockets turned out, as if someone had robbed him.

Officer Toaz had been in Charlotte all day at the Compton murder trial and returned to Grand Ledge around nine o'clock in the evening. He had met with Sheriff Sloan and was reported to have been in good spirits. He also spoke with a neighbor across the street, who reported the same. He returned home about 12:30, according to his wife.

Implications

When asked about the reported suicide of Toaz and its impact on the Compton trial, Prosecuting Attorney Peters told the *Detroit Press*: "I don't see how the suicide of Constable Toaz can interfere with the Compton trial. He was not an important witness, and the prosecution did not depend on his testimony."

The defense attorneys for Compton made sure the jury knew of Toaz's untimely death and the rumors that he had committed suicide, implying he took his own life because of guilt in the case.

The defense further presented an alibi for Compton on the night of the murder, when George Clark, another blacksmith, placed him in Eagle one hour before the murder was alleged to have occurred in Grand Ledge. Eagle and Grand Ledge were five miles apart, a distance that would take more than an hour to travel at that time.

Further strengthening his defense, Silas Compton took the stand on June 30. As he did so, the packed audience in the courtroom went silent. He denied that he ever played a card game with the Butcher brothers, which was where the alleged plan to rob Lampman was supposed to have been hatched. John Butcher had testified that it was over a poker game they decided to kill Lampman. Compton also denied that he had been hiding in Pennsylvania, stating he had nothing to fear, as he was not involved in any way with the murder or robbery of Lampman.

Verdict

On July 2, 1907, the jury went into deliberation. They returned just short of five hours later, and the court was still filled with a crowd of people eager to hear the outcome.

The final defense testimony from George Clark, and Silas Compton himself, had profoundly affected the decision of the jury. The twelve men voted for acquittal.

The older Compton partially broke down in grief when hearing the verdict. Not losing a moment's time, he walked over to the jury and shook each of their hands. Although he had many invitations from friends to stay at their homes now that he was free, Compton refused and returned to stay at the cell in the county jail for the night before returning to his home in Pennsylvania the next day.

When Compton was asked by a reporter about the death of Officer Toaz, he admitted he blamed him for his having been arrested in the first place. However, he was unable to talk further on it due to his sorrow over the man's tragic death.

John Butcher, now that the trial was completed, was swiftly returned to the Michigan State Penitentiary in Jackson. Following this, he received even further criticism and blame for Compton's arrest.

Board of Pardons

Three years following the acquittal of Silas Compton, John Butcher went before the board of pardons in December 1910. During that time, there was a determined effort by John Butcher's sister, who remained unwavering in her belief of her brother's innocence, to obtain his release. He had maintained good behavior throughout his seventeen years of incarceration.

The State Board of Pardons reviewed his case and commuted his sentence to a term of fifty years, which allowed him to be released on parole on September 7, 1911, for good behavior. He was delivered to the home of his sister.

The citizens of Eaton County were still very much divided in opinion over his guilt or innocence when the news of his release was announced. However, when the decision was made, after eighteen years, no one raised any serious objections.

After Butcher served twenty years of his sentence, his final discharge was approved by Governor Woodbridge Ferris on May 16, 1913, when Butcher was forty-eight years old.

In Memoriam

William Lampman was buried with military honors at Oakwood Cemetery in Grand Ledge with a Civil War headstone.

Sheriff Samuel Pollock enjoyed a successful public life, serving as not only county sheriff but also county supervisor, city alderman and streets commissioner. He was an active member of the Grand Army of the Republic and passed away following a heart attack at the age of sixty-three in May 1904. He is buried at Maple Hill Cemetery in Charlotte.

The death of Thomas J. Toaz in 1907 at the age of fifty-six drew law enforcement from all over the state to assist with the investigation of his death. No suspects were ever identified. The coroner's jury that investigated his death was undecided whether it was murder or suicide. His death remains an unsolved mystery. He is also buried in Oakwood Cemetery.

John Butcher remained a free man until his death on April 8, 1948, at the age of eighty-two. He was interred at the North Eagle Cemetery.

8

DARK NIGHT IN NILES

(1892)

There was a great ringing of bells and tooting of horns, firing of guns and pyrotechnics, when the first train pulled into the little village…followed by much "passing of the rosy" in the figurative language.
—Niles Weekly Mirror, *February 24, 1892*

It was on October 25, 1848, when the woodland banks of the St. Joseph River near Niles, Michigan, echoed for the first time the iconic puffing and blowing followed by the shrill whistles of the locomotive engine. The Michigan Central Railroad line from Detroit to Niles had finally completed its westward expansion, which began as an ambitious idea in 1832.

The extension of the railroad to Niles marked the most important epoch in the history of the town, as the new, rapid and cheap transportation stimulated commerce and every industry, bringing with it increases in population and prosperity. Four years later, another surge followed when the tracks were completed all the way to Chicago, sparking forty years of constant improvement in the railroad and its facilities.

The Depot

The first passenger train depot in Niles was constructed before the arrival of the first steam engine. This structure burned to the ground in October

Niles Train Depot, circa 1875. *Library of Michigan.*

1873. The Michigan Central immediately began to draw up plans for a larger station but, in the meantime, constructed a convenient temporary structure within five days. It was intended to serve one year, with the vision of breaking ground on a more commodious structure soon after.

Through ill fortune, the company struggled in the years following the erection of this makeshift depot, enduring poor management challenges as well. Contrary to the expectations of the community, the temporary station remained for eighteen years in Niles as an unsightly, small and cramped facility.

Finally, in 1890, the railroad purchased approximately six acres from various landowners in the city and broke ground on a new station. This new depot was constructed in a Richardsonian Romanesque style of architecture, built of heavy Carroll brown sandstone from Ohio, rough in finish and warm in its reddish amber tones. The depot was officially opened to the public on February 8, 1892, and offered a spacious transportation terminal that became admired across the state.

The interior was finished in terra-cotta walls contrasted by polished oak, ornamental brass, tall plate-glass windows and beautiful artwork over a central fireplace across from the ticket office. The facility was complete with separate men and women's waiting rooms; restrooms; a dining room, including upstairs apartments for the management and restaurant staff; and a telegraph office. The exterior boasted high hipped and gabled roofs and a square tower with a magnificent clock displaying five-foot dials brightly illuminated at night and visible from a considerable distance. Altogether, the new building combined architectural beauty with the harmony of perfect taste in décor and design.

The opening of the new station in 1892 was an upgrade, grander in scale and appearance than most small-town train depots. The railroad's plan was deliberate, as they designed it to impress cross-country travelers on their way to the World's Columbian Exposition to be held in Chicago in 1893. With a desire to make this new depot even more spectacular, the Michigan Central hired renowned German landscape gardener John Gipner to supervise and maintain the station's gardens, along with the gardens at ten other stations on the line.

In 1893, Gipner began the practice of having every woman passenger presented with a rose or carnation, each with a special tag that read "Compliments of the Michigan Central Railroad," employing six young flower boys in blue uniforms adorned with bellboy-style hats to hand out the floral tributes. Although Gipson managed gardens at many stations, none along the line were as beautiful as the one in Niles. As a result, Niles soon became known as the Garden City. For years, hearing the conductors announce "Niles next stop" would result in passengers clamoring to the windows to get a glimpse of the depot and its gardens.

Today the Niles train station is listed on the National Register of Historic Places, and the gardens are maintained by a local garden club. It has served as a filming location for three Hollywood films. Steven Spielberg's

Niles Depot Grand Opening, 1892. *Niles History Center.*

Niles Station rendering, 1892. *From the* Niles Weekly Mirror, *February 24, 1892.*

first project with Amblin Entertainment in 1981, *Continental Divide*, starring John Belushi and Blair Brown, used the depot as a location. Later, the 1988 action comedy *Midnight Run* starring Robert De Niro and Charles Grodin used it in a scene. Finally, the 1991 film *Only the Lonely*, starring John Candy, Maureen O'Hara, Ally Sheedy and Anthony Quinn, decorated the station with Christmas lights for filming. Since that year, the depot has maintained that tradition by being decorated with lights from the first of December through Christmas.

In 1892, the depot was not the only improvement the Michigan Central Railroad built. The project included a viaduct crossing the tracks with a steel truss bridge, connecting Fifth Street with the station. Additionally, Second Street was lowered in grade to allow for easy access under the tracks through a new sandstone archway. Both of these new construction projects augmented public access to the railroad station on either side of the tracks.

These improvements, along with the depot, were opened with much fanfare on that cold February day in 1892. No one in attendance could ever envision, much less foresee, the sinister crime that would be committed directly across the tracks from this beautiful new edifice later that same year, an incident that would shake the community more soundly than the largest locomotive.

Screams at Dusk

The switch engine and crew were at work in the railroad yard near the Niles Depot at 5:50 p.m. on Wednesday evening, December 7, 1892, when John Etzcorn, the yard master, heard the echo of a pistol shot, followed by a scream. The sound was coming from the direction of Mary Comley's residence across the tracks. Uncertain about what he had heard, he called another worker, John Walker, along with Engineer Charles Johnson over from the switch engine. The three men listened intently, and they soon heard another scream followed by a cry for help. Someone was in trouble.

Etzcorn and Johnson started in the direction of the house by way of the Fifth Street viaduct bridge carrying lanterns. When they reached the other side, they met Henry Pateman, another railroad worker, who joined them. Along the way, they encountered Chris Ream heading to his repair shop on a cross street. He had also heard the gunshot but expressed uncertainty if the noise he heard was an animal or made by a person. Ream continued on his way to work, and the three men continued up the street.

When the railroad men reached the Comley house on North Sixth Street, Patemen knocked on the kitchen door. They received no response.

Etzcorn called out "Mary?" but no reply came. They stood in silence for a few moments, listening intently. Inside the house was dark. The men stood on the porch with the aid of lanterns—still, no movement within the

SECOND STREET ARCHWAY AT NILES.

Stone Archway. *From the* Niles Weekly Mirror, *February 24, 1892.*

Viaduct. *From the* Niles Weekly Mirror, *February 24, 1892.*

home could be discerned. No footsteps. No voices. No identification of life. Nothing broke the silence.

Pateman knocked again and then tried the door latch. It was unlocked. After a momentary pause, he looked at his companions. Etzcorn and Johnson nodded. With a turn of the latch, Pateman opened the door.

When the glow of the lanterns shone within, the trio recoiled in horror.

Mary Comley

Mary Comley was born in 1834, the daughter of Joshua and Elizabeth Comley. Her parents had moved to the Michigan territory from Ohio in 1832, being among the first families to settle in Niles. She was the first in her family born in their newly chosen home.

The Comleys owned a large parcel of farmland in the center of Niles, across from where the new train station now stood. After her parents died, the land passed to her brother John. The city of Niles grew up around them, dividing into smaller lots, but the Comleys kept their land whole and undivided as a farm. Mary never married and stayed living with her older brothers Ephriam and John and their families. Her two other brothers, Milton and David, moved away to other counties in Michigan.

Her sister Hester married Amable LaPierre in 1840 and moved to South Bend, Indiana. Amable LaPierre became an active conductor on the

Underground Railroad for two decades in northwest Indiana and southwest Michigan prior to the Civil War, suffering personal and financial hardships transporting people escaping enslavement to Canada. Amable and Hester moved back to Niles in 1852 and became an integral part of the community. For many years, the couple took charge of the Michigan Central restaurant at the depot, serving food to thousands of travelers to and from Chicago, as well as local residents.

The Comley family was considered wealthy, as land values increased in Niles. Being so close to the train depot, although seemingly a convenient asset, their home was burglarized on a few occasions by transient thieves traveling the Michigan Central line.

On one occasion, in 1887, a nephew and former employee of John Comley broke into their home and stole over $300. The thief, George Taylor, was eventually arrested, found guilty of larceny and sent to prison at the Ionia Penitentiary for two years. At the trial, both John and Mary testified against him.

In 1888, thieves again broke in and stole jewelry and other money when Mary was not at home, and this time the culprits were never caught. Living alone on her land, with no close neighbors for safety, grew as a concern for Mary following this incident.

Ephriam Comley died in 1885. When John began to experience poor health in 1887, he added Mary onto the deed of the land. John passed away a

Niles Depot with train, circa 1895. *Niles History Center*.

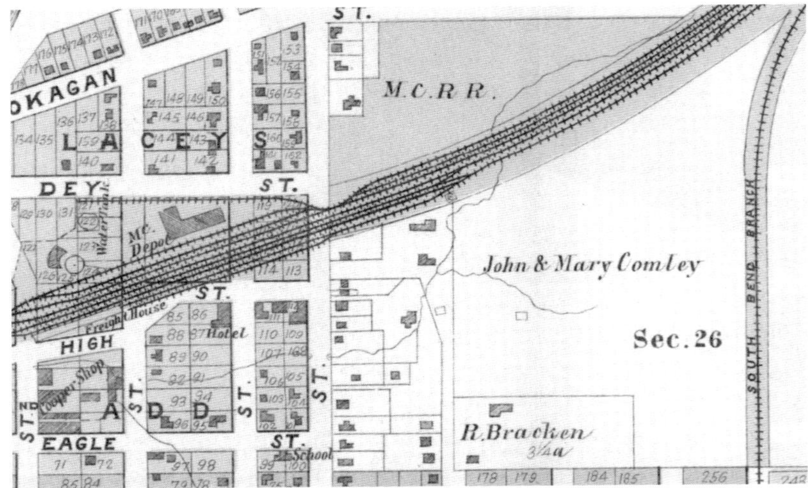

An 1887 Atlas showing Comley property in Niles. *W.W. Graves Rand McNally & Co., 1887.*

year later, and Mary became sole owner of the large Comley property in section 26, in the heart of the city.

When the Michigan Central Railroad announced their proposal for the improvements of the depot and viaduct in 1890, Mary for the first time announced she would divide some of her land into lots to build cottages to make more homes available for people moving into the area. The move was praised by the newspapers, as it offered much-needed housing for the growing city.

Mary brought suit against the Michigan Central in February 1892, a week before the grand opening of the new depot, for trespassing on her land. She was awarded $300 in a settlement with the company.

Mary Comley was fifty-nine years old and an active member of the Methodist Episcopal Church. She and her sister Hester were revered in the city. Selling these new lots had the added benefit of closer neighbors, which gave Mary some comfort.

When John Etzcorn, Henry Patemen and Charles Johnson opened the door to Mary Comley's home that December evening in 1892, nothing could prepare them for what they were about to see. They gasped in unison.

Horror Unprecedented

The radiance of the lantern revealed, directly opposite the door they had entered, a large pool of blood on the floor near the stove. To the right of this, about two or three feet away, was another. At the end of the distant dining room was yet another smaller crimson circle.

A lamp had been knocked over in front of the stove, and lamp oil was sprayed about. The woman's false teeth lay on the opposite side of the room. Visible drag marks streaked vermillion lines through the pools toward a storeroom at the far end of the room. Protruding out of a doorway leading to this room lay the feet and legs of Mary Comley.

Someone had clearly dragged her body to the storeroom doorway. A singular streak of blood left a trail to the body. Inside the storeroom, a stairway led to the cellar. Mary was found in a sitting position, leaning against the wall near the top of the stairs, dark stains of blood mixed with lamp oil down the front of her dress. The killer had also exited through the same kitchen door moments before the three men arrived, leaving bloody handprints on the latch handle. Somehow in the fading light he had managed to leave no visible footprints.

Underneath Mary's body, when examined later, lay a .32-caliber pistol, with the handle broken. Two cartridges had misfired, and the third was vacant. The fired shot had struck the rear living room wall. A mop and a broom covered with blood were found near the stove, with clear handprints in blood on the kitchen table. Also found beneath the victim was a buggy whip.

Her throat had been cut from the center windpipe to about half an inch below the right and left ears, obviously from a sharp knife, severing the jugular vein. Another large laceration was found on her scalp above her right ear, extending three inches backward. She also bore marks of having been beaten with the butt end of the revolver like a club. If the other wounds and bruises on her face were not enough to have killed her, the fractures to her skull, with two fresh indentations in a round shape exposing brain matter, certainly were. The gruesome scene was horror unprecedented for the small community of Niles.

The Investigation Begins

The police were notified immediately. Sheriff Charles Alfred Johnson arrived at nine o'clock that evening, and Deputy U.S. Marshal William

Alonzo Palmer arrived about an hour later from Buchanan, Michigan. The killer had quite the head start by the time they made it to the scene. Not only was it dark, but it had begun to rain as well. Word spread throughout the city, and the level of excitement quickly grew. Few, if any, in Niles were able to sleep that night.

When Berrien County Marshal Robert Shilladay arrived at the house, he looked at the scene and started out into the town to bring in every man who could not account for his presence that day. The initial theory he was operating on was that whichever brute had committed this crime, his clothing would give evidence of his actions, as there was no way anyone could have left there without blood all over them. Deputies combed the city collecting men.

In all, the marshal rounded up fourteen strong men that evening by eleven o'clock, but he found no evidence that any of that lot had a hand in the crime.

Meanwhile, the coroner appointed a jury consisting of George Forler, Lew Hoyt, Thomas Dean, Charles Radwald, Benjamin Earl and Elvin Fox. The body was moved to the upstairs room, where Dr. Simeon Belknap made his examination of the deceased and wrapped her wounds as best he could.

Close inspection of the scene revealed that the attack on Mary Comley apparently occurred right when she returned from the meat market after purchasing some beef, which was found lying on the counter. She had been sitting at the kitchen table, having dinner. The shot was heard shortly after the killer burst in upon her.

He likely knocked on the door, and when she came to answer, he fired his gun and missed. The bullet hit the wall on the far side of the room, and that was when Mary screamed. The killer pulled the trigger twice more, but the gun misfired both rounds. Mary grabbed the nearest weapon available to her, which was her buggy whip that she had placed on the counter, and began striking him. When she fell to the floor, Mary fought back, knocking over a mop and broom that had been leaning against the counter. In her desperation to fight off her assailant, she grabbed the handles of each to strike him.

The killer overpowered her, attacking with the butt end of the gun. He beat her around the head and face, knocking over the kerosene lamp on the kitchen table. When Mary lost consciousness, he dragged her toward the storeroom, intent on depositing her body in the cellar and perhaps setting fire to the house to conceal the crime.

While being pulled across the floor of the darkened house, she likely regained consciousness, resuming her struggle, whereupon he dropped the gun and held her throat against the wall to prevent her from screaming again. Pulling a knife from his pocket, he cut her throat.

Hearing the sounds of people approaching, or perhaps just aware the noises would soon bring discovery, he left her in a sitting position against the wall. Abandoning his plans of putting her body in the cellar, he exited through the kitchen door and ran off into the night.

Suspects Hunted

When an inspection was made of the crime scene, the coroner's jury soon concluded that the motive was not robbery. They had taken Amable and Hester LaPierre through the home, and they avowed that there was no money or other valuables apparently missing.

Mary was not married and lived alone. Nor was she reported to be in a relationship, as confirmed by the LaPierres. Therefore, investigators quickly dismissed any suggestion of a crime of passion. Her recent settlement with the MCRR was evaluated briefly, but it could hardly be considered a motive for murder. If so, by whom? The railroad had paid similar fines in many of these types of cases across Michigan.

Without entirely ruling out a random transient psychopath, investigators surmised the motive for the murder gave the impression of being revenge. When this was suggested to the LaPierres, they quickly offered one name, and only one: George Taylor, the nephew of Mary and Hester.

George Taylor. *From the* Niles Republican, *May 4, 1893.*

When George Taylor was convicted five years earlier for the burglary at the home of John Comley, Mary had testified at his trial. She witnessed George leaving their home on the day of the robbery and stated so on the witness stand. After this testimony, George had abruptly stood up and threatened Mary Comley in the courtroom, vowing that he would kill her when he was released. George served two years in the Ionia State Reformatory for that conviction.

George Taylor was last known to be at the Michigan State Penitentiary in Jackson, having been sent there three years prior, but was now serving a four-and-a-half-year sentence on another conviction.

Hearing this story, Marshal Shilladay sent Deputy William Metcalf on the next train to the Jackson prison to ascertain whether Taylor had been released or was still in custody.

While awaiting a response from the prison officials, a brakeman from the railroad came forward, indicating they had seen George Taylor, using the name George Holtz, in the city earlier in the week, after arriving at the train depot. That same evening, a little girl told her parents that a man stopped her on the way to school that day asking for directions to Mary Comley's house. She gave a description that matched Taylor and described him as carrying what looked like a bundle of clothes.

The next day, a deputy in Centreville, Michigan, arrested a man who had blood on his face and clothing and claimed to have been in Niles the day before. They detained him for Sheriff Johnson, who sent deputies to escort the suspect to Niles. When the suspect arrived at the train station with law enforcement, a crowd of citizens gathered at the station to witness the arrival. That man did not turn out to be Taylor. After questioning, he was determined not to be a suspect and released.

George Taylor

George Taylor committed his first burglary in Marion, Indiana, at age nineteen, robbing the Spencer rooming house. He fled to Michigan, avoiding prosecution. In 1887, he was convicted of the burglary at the home of John and Mary Comley.

He was twenty-four years old when he was released from the Ionia Penitentiary on January 1, 1889. He was described by the *South Bend Tribune*:

> *Five feet, ten inches tall, and wearing a slouch hat, a rusty looking overcoat and arctic overshoes. His left eye was dead, giving him a salt mackerel stare and the other was light blue and evasive. His nose was long, with an upward tendency at the end, and below it hung a middle weight yellow moustache which partly concealed a small, weak mouth and squirrel teeth.*

Following his release from Ionia, he returned to Niles. A few weeks after his arrival, he rented a horse and buggy on January 19 from the Bunbury

Brothers Livery Stable under the pretense of going to Bertrand, Michigan, for the day. He never returned.

Instead, he drove the buggy down to Marion, Indiana, and commenced working on his father's farm. When his father had inquired as to where he had come by the horses and buggy, he told him he received them as payment in exchange for some work on a farm.

The Bunbury Brothers reported the stolen rig to Sheriff Benton R. Sterns and offered a reward for its return. Telegrams and telephone wires were used in sending dispatches in every direction, and several thousand circulars were sent through the mail, giving a full description of the stolen property and the man they described in detail as a one-eyed thief, George Taylor.

In Indiana, Sheriff Hollman located Taylor on his father's farm five days later and arrested him, returning him to Niles.

When he arrived in Niles, three hundred people showed up at the train station to get a glimpse of the prisoner in his handcuffs. Taylor shook like a leaf when they escorted him through the crowd and placed him in the carriage omnibus. The eager crowd encircled the omnibus, pushing and swaying it to and fro, and one man climbed on top. When he arrived at the jail, Taylor was fed a dinner while still trembling and then placed in his cell.

He was charged the next day with larceny for stealing the horses. Although his defense attorney worked diligently to have the charges dropped, his prior conviction history for burglary was a hindrance and helped seal his fate. When convicted at trial this time, he was sentenced to serve four and a half years in the Michigan State Prison in Jackson.

He again blamed Mary Comley for that outcome.

REWARD OFFERED

The day after Deputy Metcalf traveled to Jackson, he telegrammed back to Marshal Shilladay informing him Taylor had been released from prison the Thursday before. He was let out early for good behavior. The prison officials informed the deputy that Taylor was also known to use the alibi George Holtz.

The manhunt for Taylor was launched, with notifications sent to surrounding communities in Michigan and Indiana. A few weeks later, a $500 reward was offered for his arrest by the Berrien County Board of Supervisors.

Lobby of Niles Train Station, 2024. *Author collection.*

C.W. Pegg, a reporter for the *Goshen Times* in Indiana, received a picture of George Taylor. Sheriff Elliott Crull of Elkhart, Indiana, sent in the image. Believing the face looked familiar, Pegg went to Charles Irwin's icehouse, where he thought he had seen this man working using the name Albert Smith. Pegg observed him for a time and became convinced it was Taylor. He secretly followed the suspect to where he was staying at Irwin's and sleeping in his barn.

The reporter then went to report the discovery to Sheriff Crull, who assigned Deputy Frank Kidder to investigate. Meanwhile, a postman in Goshen, Indiana, who had also received a card with the photo of the fugitive, spotted Taylor and reported him. Sheriff Kidder went there to follow up on the report and ultimately arrested the man claiming to be Albert Smith at the home of Charles Irwin, retaining him at the Goshen jail on Friday, January 13, 1893.

Following the arrest, Sheriff Crull notified Marshal Shilladay at Niles. Shilladay traveled by sleigh directly to the jail in Goshen with Edward LaPierre, the nephew of Mary Comley, and Berrien County Deputy Benjamin F. Earl. The suspect was brought out, and LaPierre said on first sight, "That is Taylor."

In response, Taylor said, "No, my name is Smith."

To further confirm his identification, Marshal Shilladay contacted Ed Powers, formerly of Niles. He used to work at the Hotel Haskel, which Taylor was known to frequent, and now lived in Goshen. Powers confirmed Taylor's identify, later stating, "I know Taylor, and knew him when I first saw him."

After tending to the horses, Deputy Earl stepped into the room after Powers had spoken and also identified Taylor. The deputy had been involved with the arrest of George Taylor for stealing the horses three years before. Confronted with this, the man claiming to be Albert Smith acquiesced and confirmed he was George Taylor.

Initially, Taylor refused to go back to Michigan, requesting an official requisition from the governor. Deputy Earl talked to him privately and persuaded him to waive this, and he agreed to return. After being held overnight in Goshen, Taylor was escorted back to the Niles jail. The *South Bend Tribune* acknowledged that Marshal Shilladay was concerned about crowds becoming violent, fearing the attempted administration of "lynch law," but reported: "They took every precaution possible under the circumstances. They approached Niles by a circuitous route, and once inside the city drove their horses on a dead run to the lockup."

When they reached the jail, crowds of men and boys swarmed from every direction. Deputy Earl, who was handcuffed to Taylor, dragged him inside the station. The following day, Taylor was transferred without incident to Berrien Springs to await trial.

Further investigation revealed that when Taylor was released from prison he was wearing an overcoat, but that was not on him when he was arrested. In March, another former inmate of the Jackson prison who was released at the same time as Taylor and met him in Goshen came forward. He had in his possession an overcoat that Taylor had exchanged with him. When the coat was finally surrendered to Deputy Sheriff Kidder, it was revealed to have blood in several places, including inside the pockets. Also inside one of the pockets was a letter addressed to Taylor, along with a photograph. These items were added to the photographic evidence of the crime scene, and Taylor was charged with murder.

THE TRIAL

The trial was held in Berrien Springs at the County Courthouse in May 1893. The court appointed attorney William Campbell Hicks of Benton

Harbor to defend George Taylor, while Prosecuting Attorney Edward L. Hamilton from Niles appeared on behalf of the people. Judge James O'Hara from St. Joseph presided over the trial.

During the trial, George Taylor's checkered career was detailed, including his two prison terms in Ionia and Jackson.

When questioned, Taylor denied having been in Niles that day, claiming he had been working in Goshen since his release from prison. However, several witnesses testified to having seen him in town. In addition to the railroad worker and the little schoolgirl, there was also a hotel representative who came forward, showing evidence that Taylor registered for a room in Niles the day of the murder.

The investigators also confirmed that Taylor had arrived in Goshen on December 8, the day after the murder, and obtained a job from a grocer carrying potatoes down to the cellar, for which he was paid one dollar. The grocer soon after got him a job delivering coal and ice with Charles Irwin and made arrangements for him to sleep at night in Irwin's barn. This was where he was found at the time of his arrest. The grocer and Irwin both testified, confirming this timeline.

Another witness included George Hicks, who knew Taylor in prison. He claimed he heard Taylor openly talking about getting revenge on Mary Comley. Hicks advised him to not retaliate against the woman, telling him that serving two terms in prison should be enough. Taylor insisted that Comley had sent him to prison by swearing falsely against him, and he said, "I shall never be satisfied until I get even with that woman." Hicks admitted to pointing out to Taylor at a later time a secondhand store in Jackson, where he purchased the revolver.

A Jackson pawn broker named Norris testified to selling a pistol to Taylor. He confirmed it was the same revolver found at the scene.

Thomas Beckas, an ex-convict in Goshen, Indiana, swore Taylor wanted him to go with him to Niles on the day of the murder. Frank Shrock gave evidence of his encountering Taylor later that same evening in Goshen and hearing him talk about his long walk back from Niles.

Finally, a Mrs. Francis from Kalamazoo testified that Taylor had rented a room from her a week before; he mentioned he was looking for work and wanted to go to Niles to get even with a woman.

The evidence of the bloody coat, along with his prior threats against Mary Comley in the courtroom in 1887, were also presented as evidence against him. His clothes contained blood on them and were verified by witnesses to be the ones he was seen wearing the day of the murder.

The jury was sent into deliberation at seven o'clock on May 10 and returned two hours later with a verdict of guilty of murder in the first degree. Judge O'Hara asked Taylor if he had anything to say, and he responded, "I have not, but think the people were not honest with me."

Judge O'Hara then sentenced him to life in prison at hard labor in the Michigan State Penitentiary in Jackson. Taylor hung his head with an expression of unconcern and was led out of the courtroom.

THE LAPIERRE FAMILY

Mary Comley died leaving no will, and her property was transferred to her surviving sister Hester in probate. She was buried in Silverbrook Cemetery.

Amable LaPierre passed away at the age of eighty from cancer of the stomach on March 27, 1894. Hester LaPierre passed away four weeks later in April at the age of seventy-one. They had been married over fifty-four years. The family property eventually passed to their daughter Eva La Pierre and her husband, George Egbert.

Amable and Hester's son Edward LaPierre owned and operated a successful jewelry business in Niles. Edward had testified at the trial of

LaPierre headstone, Silverbrook Cemetery, Niles, Michigan. *Author collection.*

George Taylor, and during the trial, Taylor threatened his life as well. A few years earlier, two men tried to rob his jewelry store and they were apprehended. Edward testified at their trial, sending them both to prison. These men also vowed to get even with him.

Following the death of his aunt, Edward brooded quite often about his business. In truth, he lived in constant fear that Taylor or the two men would make an attempt on his life, either by obtaining release or by using proxy. As a result, after the death of both his parents, he spent many evenings walking in Silverbrook Cemetery. Sometimes he sat by their graves alone late into the night to quell his mood.

On Friday, November 29, 1895, Edward said goodbye to his son, Guy LaPierre, upon leaving the store for the evening. He stopped by the homes of a few friends. One of these friends, Henry Lardner, contacted Guy later that evening while he was still at the store, expressing concern that Edward seemed particularly agitated when he left. Worried, Guy collected a family friend, Dr. Lowell Clark, and together they went to Silverbrook Cemetery. They first visited the LaPierre family grave site, but Edward was not there. Driving to the north side of the cemetery, they found Edward on top of some steps, lifeless, with both hands crossed over his chest. There was a visible bullet hole in his right temple, and his right hand grasped the butt of a .38-caliber revolver. His death was investigated and ruled a suicide.

Guy LaPierre continued running the jewelry business for several years, while at the same time attending school to learn multiple languages. He sold the jewelry business in 1906 and took a position as a foreign representative for the Kellogg Food Corporation, moving to New York City. He retired in 1942 and passed away in Battle Creek in 1952.

AFTERMATH

In June 1893, the $500 reward for the arrest of George Taylor was disbursed evenly between Deputy Sheriff Hiram "Frank" Kidder from Elkhart County, who went to Goshen to investigate, and the mail carrier who reported him.

The first efforts by George Taylor to secure release began in 1895. He wrote letters to various officials in the city of Niles and across the state, protesting his innocence. The rambling letters accused other parties of the crime but offered no clear evidence. The only attorney who would help him with an appeal was William C. Hicks who had defended him in the original trial. Although Hicks believed Taylor was innocent, his efforts to obtain a pardon that year failed.

In July 1903, George Taylor petitioned the State Board of Pardons for release. He again claimed innocence of the crime, maintaining law enforcement had accused the wrong man. The board met in Niles to review the evidence in his case. William A. Palmer, a former marshal, who had served as an undersheriff for Berrien County during the time of the Taylor case, testified before the board assuring them that there was not the slightest doubt they had properly convicted the guilty man. The board held their official meeting in March 1904 and, after review, denied Taylor's petition.

In November 1905, Grace Raypholtz, a wealthy niece of George Taylor from Marion, Indiana, agreed to commit $30,000 to help him gain his freedom. She hired F.T. Hartzell, a private investigator, to look into his case. The investigator managed to get all of the members of the original coroner's jury still living to sign a document recommending that his life sentence be commuted to a shorter term. Hartzell wrote a report to the Board of Pardons stating Taylor had been convicted entirely on circumstantial evidence and that his behavior in prison had been exemplary.

Niles Train Station, 2024. *Author collection.*

Additionally, Hartzell included a letter presenting his version of a plausible theory for alternate suspects. The letter accused the LaPierre family of the crime, declaring Mary Comley had threatened to bequeath her property to an unnamed boy who was living with her, cutting the LaPierres out of the estate. This claim sparked a storm of protest and outrage from citizens in Niles who knew Mary Comley and the LaPierre family. Investigation revealed there was no such boy living with Mary. Probate records verified she died intestate. The letters and refuting evidence were reviewed by the board of pardons and sent to Governor Frederick M. Warner on November 30. The governor denied the petition.

In 1910, the Michigan state legislature passed a new law that allowed prisoners serving life sentences to be eligible for parole after serving twenty-five years. Prisoners with good behavior records could have additional time credited, reducing their sentence to less than twenty-five years. Applications required parole board approval, with a final requisite signature by the governor.

George Taylor petitioned again in 1911 and 1913. Both were denied.

In April 1914, Taylor submitted to the board of pardons another application for commuting his sentence from life in prison to twenty-five years. If the petition was granted, he would be released in May 1915. At the hearing, no one from Niles appeared on Taylor's behalf. Guy LaPierre, the nephew of Mary Comley, spoke at the hearing opposing his release. Taylor's petition was denied. He petitioned the governor in January 1915, and this was also denied.

In January 1916, after serving twenty-three years, Taylor was again before the parole board, requesting to be paroled early under the new law, on the grounds of good behavior. Governor Woodbridge Ferris personally visited the Michigan State Prison in Jackson to interview several prisoners but declined to interview Taylor. Governor Ferris paroled only two convicts in 1916, and Taylor was not one of them.

In December 1919, Taylor petitioned again. This time his interview passed to the next level of review. He passed this interview on April 4, 1920, and was advanced to the final examination by the board of pardons on July 23. He was directed by the board on August 12 to file an application for clemency, detailing what his plans would be if granted parole. Taylor submitted this application, which described how he intended to move to Pocatello, Idaho, if released. His petition for parole was approved by Governor Albert Sleeper on September 22, and he was discharged from prison on September 27, 1920.

9

MAD MINNIE HERRE

(1893)

One very strange circumstance connected with the affair is that just a few hours previous to the death of Mrs. Herre's son, two pigs and a calf died in terrible agony.

—Lansing State Journal, *May 18, 1893*

Frank and Minnie Herre were born and raised in Bamberg, Poland. In the late 1860s, Poland gave up its independence, submitting to Russian rule. With increasing oppression under Russian control, it was not long after that the Poles had several failed national uprisings. In 1871, the German Empire was established, and they also sought control of the Polish territory. By the early 1870s, Poland was caught between the international forces of Russia and Germany and its national identity appeared to be headed toward eradication.

Immigrants

Only fluent in their native language of Polish, the Herres made the decision, as did so many others in their time, to seek relief from the oppressive environment in their homeland and immigrate to the United States in the early 1870s. With designs on a new beginning, they purchased a forty-acre farm in Meridian Township just south of Okemos, Michigan. Frank worked at improving his fluency in English in earnest, while Minnie chose to remain close to the farm, relying on her husband to engage with others in their newly adopted home.

In 1878, their first child, a daughter they named Pauline, was born. A few years later, in 1881, another daughter, Emma, was born, followed by a son in 1884, whom they named George.

To their surprise, in 1888 they had a set of twin sons, whom they named Walter and James. Tragically, the twin boys both died less than a year later, one month apart. James passing away in July and Walter in August. For Minnie, the loss of the twins was unbearable, and she mourned their death for over a year.

In 1891, tragedy struck again. Frank was killed by a falling tree while out working on their property. Minnie was now a widow with three young children trying to manage a farm on her own. The struggle was even more compounded, as she habitually relied on her husband in matters of business and forewent acquiring a command of English. Frank had long been her anchor of stability, and she found life in his absence insufferable.

Strange Demise

Minnie attempted to manage the farm, but the day-to-day toils under the burden of loss was miserable. In time, the numbers of livestock dwindled, gradually dying off from lack of proper care, and the farmhouse too became neglected. Despite assistance from the children, Minnie found life in Michigan inhospitable and difficult.

On Saturday, May 13, 1893, little George Herre began complaining he had a stomachache, and his condition grew rapidly worse. In the middle of the night, Dr. James W. Ferguson was summoned to their house by his mother. Following an examination, the doctor prescribed some medicine for him. By Sunday, George was feeling much better, and by Monday, he had all but entirely recovered.

That evening, however, he became sick again. Early Tuesday morning, on May 16, he went into convulsions and abruptly died from apparent heart failure. Dr. Ferguson found the sudden death of the boy to be strange and told Minnie Herre he recommended a postmortem examination. Minnie, however, objected to this, informing the doctor she would not allow it.

An 1874 Atlas of Meridian Township, Okemos, showing the Herre farm. *Library of Congress.*

Funeral services for George were scheduled for two days hence in the morning at the Okemos Baptist Church. The doctor was not willing to accept the mandate from Minnie Herre and visited Prosecuting Attorney Henry Gardener. He explained his concerns and professional desire to conduct an autopsy on the boy. Gardner agreed and ordered the postmortem examination to be conducted the following morning. The scheduled funeral was therefore delayed until the afternoon.

Sitting up with the Dead

During the 1800s, a death vigil with the body of the deceased was common, although in present day, it is mostly associated with Appalachian tradition in the United States. Before a burial of a loved one, the custom consisted of sitting up all night with relatives in the deceased's home. Often neighbors and churchgoers would bring food, coffee and tea to the family in mourning and join in the ritual.

The tradition extends back centuries in many cultures around the world, and the purpose for this practice was twofold. One, in case the person was just in a coma, they wanted to be sure someone was there to notify the doctor should they awaken. The other reason was more practical: guarding the body from rodents in the nighttime hours before burial. Some cultures kept incense sticks burning all night for this purpose to mask the smell of decomposition.

On the night before the funeral, Minnie Herre and her two daughters, Pauline, aged sixteen, and Emma, aged eleven, were attending to visiting neighbors. Minnie told her guests on several occasions that she needed to step outside to get some air, stating she was not feeling well. Her frequent departures from the small gathering therefore raised no concerns from sympathetic visitors, much less suspicions.

The body of little George lay alone on a wooden board suspended by two stools in the back room. Most of the gathering was in the front living room of the home, where visitors lingered and conversed. Around two o'clock in the morning, the two daughters found themselves sitting alone with two neighbors, Rosalind Guile and Adelia Johnson. All of the other guests had departed, and their mother had just reentered the house after being outside for a time.

The five women engaged in quiet conversation. Then they suddenly heard a loud crash in the back bedroom, followed by the sound of broken glass shattering on the floor interrupting the silence of their late-night vigil. Their mother, who had been standing near the bedroom door, jumped back with surprise.

Pauline and Emma, sitting together in the low candlelight, looked at the other women in surprise. A draft of wind from the back room caused the candles in the room to flicker, and a few blew out. Immediately, Pauline stood up and grabbed a lit candle. Together with Emma she proceeded toward the bedroom, while their mother and the other two women followed close behind.

When they approached the open door to the bedroom, the light was extinguished almost immediately. A steady cool night wind was now blowing through the open and broken window as they stood in complete darkness.

Leaning close in together, the women waited in the dark listening for about five minutes before Pauline hesitantly relit the candle with a match from the pocket in her dress and proceeded into the bedroom. To their horror, when they entered the room, the curtains were billowing from the open window and George was no longer lying on the board. Nor was he anywhere in the room.

His body had been stolen!

Search and Suspicions

Pauline and Emma immediately ran out of the room, collecting Johnson and Guile, and went to a neighboring house, where they alerted them about what had happened. Minnie remained behind in the home, declaring she was too ill to go. In the darkness of the early morning, the alarm bell was sounded. Slowly the neighbors in the village began to awaken as people assembled and joined the search.

Initially, no trace of the body snatchers or the body was discovered. For quite a while, as people hunted for clues in the early morning dark, it seemed that it would never be found. After sunrise, however, the search intensified. Eventually, around nine o'clock, someone approached a well with a lid over it on the property and opened it. Looking deep down with the assistance of morning sunlight along with someone lowering a lantern, they discovered the twisted body of George lying at the bottom.

The well was a large one, about forty feet deep, and situated about twenty feet from the house. One of the boards in the lid had been removed, and the corpse had been slid between to fall headlong down the shaft.

Through concerted efforts, the body was eventually brought to the surface. His limbs were tangled in an old harness that had been discarded in the well. The head of the boy had now been cut where it had struck the tile on the shaft in its downward flight.

After the body of the boy had been recovered, suspicions among the neighbors began to foment. Justice of the Peace Augustus L. Sturges was summoned, and surveying the scene, he immediately began to question Minnie Herre.

In his interrogation, he learned that on the Saturday before her son took ill, she had sent to Williamston for a box of Rough on Rats poison, along with a bottle of chloroform. She said she had used the rat poison in the barn and the chloroform for a toothache.

When questioned whether the rat poison was in a place where the boy could get at it, she responded that it was not. Asserting she only used the poison in the chicken coop, the rest remaining in the box out of George's reach, she handed it to Judge Sturges.

A later inspection of the barn revealed no traces of the poison.

STRANGE EVENTS

The appearance and condition of the little weather-beaten farmhouse and yard where the Herre family resided was considered unsightly in comparison to the thrift and tidiness of their neighbors. Evincing poverty, weeds and grass grew unheeded around the doorstep, the barn doors were crooked and on a slant, window panes were broken. A tread on the porch steps had long since collapsed, only to be replaced with an old wooden box, now being used to enter the home.

The interior of the little farm cottage contained nothing but the barest necessities. One large room served as the living room, kitchen and parlor, furnished with a cookstove, several old wooden-bottom chairs and an old bed used as a sofa. Adjoining the main room was the bedroom, where the remains of the boy now rested again on the board. A pantry separated by a stairway led to the floor above, where more bedrooms were found. There was no carpeting on the floor, and few pictures adorned the walls.

In the two years following Frank Herre's death, strange depredations had been committed at the farm. On one occasion, all of the tails had been cut off the cows. Another time the wagon wheels had been removed and been found on top of the barn, and even some stock were found killed.

Minne Herre had complained to authorities in Okemos, but after investigation, the marauders were never found. According to Minnie, life on the farm had become so unbearable that she had moved into the village for a time, only returning to the farm two months prior to little George's death.

Another strange occurrence was when two pigs and a calf suddenly died screaming in agony just a few hours before her son passed away. Their remains had been left lying in the barnyard. On hearing the news of their deaths, Dr. Ferguson ordered them removed for examination and necropsies performed.

Minne was described as being about forty years old, hair black, eyes gray and of a medium height. Her complexion was dark and her face furrowed with the marks of years of toil and worry. When interviewed by the judge and doctor, Minnie replied in broken English, exhibiting great earnestness, with light in her eyes as if enduring a mental torture.

Rough on Rats advertisement. *From the* Detroit Evening Times, *November 13, 1908.*

Confession

Following the examination by Judge Sturges, Detective Warren S. Abels from Okemos arrived on the scene and arrested Minnie Herre. Arriving at the courthouse, she soon after confessed to the crime of murdering her son. She detailed engaging a neighboring farmer, John Hasbrook, to purchase the poison on Saturday when he went to town, telling him her chicken coop was overrun with vermin.

She admitted to using it to kill the boy, as she was afraid he would grow up to be a thief. She claimed that she did not administer it to him until Sunday noon, when they had apple pie and she dosed his piece with the poison.

She explained that she gave him the poison only once, claiming he had been a bad boy. George had admitted to her that he had stolen some nails from a store in Okemos once, and that was all. It was clear from the interview that she also had designs on doing the same to her oldest daughter, Pauline, as she described her as being a bad girl just like George.

Following this, she made a straightforward admission of the events on the evening the body of the boy went missing. When she had learned earlier in the day that a postmortem examination would be conducted, she knew she would be found out. During the wake the night before, she complained of sickness to explain her frequent absence from the gathering.

On one departure, she climbed into the back window and removed the body and dropped it down the well. She hid the undertaker's cloth under her dress. Returning to the house, she secreted a crock lid from the kitchen and, when all of the attendants were looking elsewhere, threw it at the window, breaking it, which led them all to believe that someone was outside.

When the women and her daughters ran for assistance at a nearby residence, Minnie remained behind, feigning sickness. Once the others had gone, she wandered over to the outhouse and threw the burial cloth down the shaft in the darkness. Back in the house, she replaced the pot lid and waited for the neighbors.

Charged

Following her confession, Minnie Herre was held in the jail in Mason, Michigan, pending an examination by doctors. She had begun to behave erratically in front of Detective Abels, and he suspected her of being insane.

The planned postmortem examination of George's remains by the doctor was never conducted following Minnie Herre's confession. A coroner's jury assembled by Justice Sturges examined the remains before burial.

Minnie Herre, after being escorted to a women's cell in the jail, sat down on the sofa within and gazed around from one to the other of the unfeeling spectators who had gathered to watch her, as if searching for a sympathetic pair of eyes. She behaved as if she was scarcely aware of the awful crime she had committed.

Reporters asked her questions, and she answered them between sobs and sighs mechanically in her broken English, while the abstract and faraway look in her eyes was almost hidden in her flowing tears. Despite her verbal engagement with the press, her seeming indifference betokened her mind was far afield.

During the night, she rested easily in her confinement, but in the morning, her demeanor demonstrated extreme nervousness. She began to repeatedly express her desire to go back to her home and children. To her guards, she seemed to be unaware that she was being held in custody to answer for the most awful and heinous crime of murdering her child.

She pleaded with Marshal Sanford in her blend of Polish and English: "Please let me go home! Nine, den can I go heim tomorrow? Vat you going to do mit me? Oh, mine poor children."

The strange depredations that were reported to have taken place at her farm in the prior two years quickly fell into two categories of consideration. One, Minnie Herre had committed these deeds in her own fits of insanity, or else farmer boys living nearby had committed them for the sake of tantalizing and disturbing her. Both theories had merit, as evidence supported both.

The recent incident of the two pigs and the calf dying became easily explained during Minnie Herre's confession. She recounted the events following giving George the poison: he vomited. She had emptied the contents of his spew into the swill pail, mixing it into the feed of the pigs and calf. This led investigators to believe she must have given George an extraordinary dose for the result to be not only his own death but the also the death of three of her stock animals.

The official inquest was conducted at the courthouse in Okemos, which drew crowds of townspeople into the small town hall to hear what was said. Fluid from the stomach of George taken during his embalming was tested at the laboratory of Agricultural College by professor of chemistry Dr. Robert Clark Kedzie. The results determined the fluids contained white arsenic, the principal ingredient in Rough on Rats poison. Professor Kedzie was the primary expert witness, along with Dr. Johnson W. Hagadorn of Lansing and Dr. James W. Ferguson of Okemos, who had both examined the deceased.

Minne Herre was to be charged with first-degree murder, but Justice P.H. Dolan, who was assigned to the case, ordered her to be examined by doctors to determine her ability to stand trial.

Following the hearing, the funeral service for George was held at three o'clock that day and his body was interred at Okemos Cemetery.

Dr. Robert Clark Kedzie. *Findagrave.com.*

Other neighbors came forward to tell the court of their encounters with Minnie Herre. One reported that the previous winter she had shown up at their house asking to borrow a shovel, stating she intended to dig up her husband. She told them that he did not die but had been buried alive, and she wanted to free him. At that point, her husband had been deceased for one and a half years.

While in the jail, she spoke gaily of her return home, imagining her husband was again alive at home caring for their children while she was away. She would then switch moods to impatience, waiting for someone to take her there. Home was a place she would never return to.

Her behavior in the jail led some to speculate it was all a clever act. It soon bore out on examination by the judge and the doctors, along with witnesses who knew her, that she was not sophisticated enough to sustain such a ruse.

While in the courtroom, when she was brought before Judge Dolan for arraignment, she walked up to the desk of the justice and deliberately sat down on the floor in a heap while she was read the charge of murder. Her eyes were dazed, and she seemed to have little reality of what the proceedings were about.

When Judge Dolan asked her if she understood the charges against her, she did not answer. When pressed, she responded excitedly, "I hurt nobody. I wrong nobody. I kill nobody." When her excitement abated, with wild eyes she gazed about the room and then began to tear her hair out in clumps from her head. Her trial was placed on the court docket for June.

Committed

Minnie Herre was held at the jail in Mason awaiting trial and appeared at one point to become lucid and clear-headed. However, by June, when the case went before another judge, her erratic behavior had returned. Following further medical examination, Judge Rollin H. Person ordered her to be committed to the Ionia state prison for the criminally insane.

When she was transported to Ionia in late June 1893, she was described as having hardly eaten anything during her long confinement in the Mason jail. Her face was haggard, and her body was shrunken as if wasted away. Her hair was matted and disheveled, and her eyes were described as having an unnatural brightness. During her time in Ionia, when visited by reporters, she was described as still tearing out her hair and clothes and giving way to fits of crazy laughter and acting like a maniac.

After Minnie was committed, kind neighbors cared for her two daughters and for a time maintained her little house on the hill. Through the years, the reminder of the terrific crimes committed there soon became too much of a bitter memory in the community. It was not long after that the home fell into disrepair and eventually total dilapidation as a place most would rather forget.

Trial

On May 3, 1894, the attending physician at Ionia wrote to the Circuit Court in Mason that Minne Herre had recovered her mind and was competent to stand trial for the crime of murder.

The prosecuting attorney, Henry Gardner, placed her case on the docket to be tried when the court convened on May 14. Due to there being over two hundred cases on the court calendar that May, her case and fifteen others were delayed until early October. The jury was selected in the *People v. Minnie Herre* by October 9, and the trial began. The courtroom filled with spectators.

The prosecuting attorney attempted to prove that she was sane at the time of the murder and only became insane after she was caught. Her defense attorney, Arthur D. Prosser, argued that she was insane throughout, citing a long history of headaches placing her in a demented state, and was therefore not responsible for her actions.

The prosecution brought nineteen witnesses, ranging from medical doctors to neighbors and other witnesses on the night of the wake when the boy's body was discarded in the well. The defense brought nine witnesses.

During the trial, Minnie Herre appeared apparently insensible to the situation. At times, when the story of the murder of George was described, she seemed to be afflicted with remorse, shedding tears in the company of her two daughters, who sat beside her. As for her own destiny pending the outcome of the trial, she appeared to care very little.

The trial lasted two days, and the attorneys completed their final arguments late in the evening on Thursday, October 11. The judge held over his instructions to the jury to begin deliberations until the morning of October 12. Once given instructions at ten o'clock in the morning, they were out only a short time before they returned with a verdict of not guilty by reason of insanity.

The judge remanded Minnie Herre to the charge of the sheriff until a conference of physicians could review her mental condition. Almost three weeks later, after an extensive review, on November 3, the commission of medical experts pronounced Minnie Herre sane, and she was discharged from custody.

Following the acquittal, the prosecuting attorney, Henry Gardner, insisted to reporters that Minnie Herre was not crazy as determined by the jury but was instead devilish. Judge Rollin H. Person, who ordered the release, stated to the *Lansing Journal* on November 16, 1894: "I hated to do it. Here the woman is sane, but is liable to have a relapse at any time, and nobody knows what she may do. I am sorry that there is no law to cover such cases, but under the statutes as they now are, I had no choice but to order her release."

Insentient Afterlife

In 1897, a reporter from the *Lansing State Republican* encountered Minnie Herre waiting at a train depot heading to Lansing. None of the other passengers seemed to recognize her.

She stated in conversation with the reporter that she had been employed for the past two years as a cook in two Milwaukee restaurants and showed him a letter of recommendation from one of her employers. She mentioned she had visited Ionia that morning and was on her way to visit her daughter in Lansing.

He described her insentient afterlife: "She appeared absolutely unconscious of the great crime she committed and was not inclined to mingle with the crowd at the station to any great extent."

The last trace of her appears in the 1900 Ionia census, which indicated she was living alone and working as a cook in that city.

10

UNHOLY LOVE

(1897)

The assassin crept up to an open window, took deliberate aim and sent a bullet through the woman's head. She died without knowing who shot her.
—The Grand Rapids Press, *October 7, 1897*

Boyne Falls, Michigan, derives its name from the falls and rapids in the nearby Boyne River. Originally known as Boyne Valley, so named by its first settler John Miller for his home in Ireland, the town was first plotted in 1873 by William Nelson and Joseph Powers. One year later, the Grand Rapids and Indiana Railroad made its way to the small community, driven by the logging industry, and the name was changed to Boyne Falls. The community began to grow with the increasing market demand for lumber. Logging camps opened up all around the surrounding valley, followed by hotels, saloons, banks and other businesses.

The lumber cut in Boyne Falls logging camps was moved by giant wheeled carts and loaded on railroad cars by manpower or steam loaders and then transported to a lumber mill in nearby Boyne City, where it was cut and loaded onto ships. Logs were also sent to a shingle mill three miles north of Boyne Falls, where logs were cut into shingles. Timber was also used throughout the Boyne Valley area to build cabins and other framed buildings as the community grew.

On a warm day in July 1889, twenty-eight-year-old George Freeman Lee married seventeen-year-old Hattie Webster in Boyne Falls. George was by trade a butcher, originally from Canada, and Hattie was a housemaid. Hattie

Loading a lumber train in northern Michigan, 1901. *Library of Congress.*

was the daughter of John Webster and Hellen Hobs, farmers in Springdale Township, Charlevoix County. Her father was also a Canadian immigrant.

In 1893, William Nelson became the first postmaster, and Boyne Falls was officially incorporated as a village.

The Road to Deception

By a chance encounter, a twenty-nine-year-old laborer from the lumber camps, William Shain, met Hattie Lee in the summer of 1895 at a social in Boyne Falls. Secretly smitten with each other, despite Hattie being married, they began seeing each other whenever George was away at work.

Their romance blossomed, so much that Hattie's marriage with George soon fell apart. Separating from George following a bitter fight, she fled into the arms of William and moved in with him. Over the months that followed, neither she nor George made efforts to file for divorce. After a few months, Hattie moved out and moved back in with her parents in Clarion, Michigan, approximately eight miles north, desiring to distance herself from William's persistent attentions.

William wanted to marry Hattie and frequently told her so when he visited her in Clarion over the next two years. On one such visit in the early autumn of 1897, he broached the subject again, giving her the sum of seventy dollars with the agreement that she would use the money to file for a divorce from George. Hattie, after considering the matter, agreed.

However, as soon as William left, Hattie made other plans. Instead of proceeding to the courthouse or to an attorney's office, she visited her friends in Boyne City, the larger community to the west of Boyne Falls. Over the next few days, she spent the money entrusted to her by William, enjoying a good time with friends. She went shopping, drank wine and bought party favors, burning through the funds. She never filed for divorce.

William learned of Hattie's deceit, word having been sent to him by a friend. Hearing the news also that Hattie was making preparations to move to the home of her sister in southern Michigan, William was crestfallen. Overwhelmed with humiliation and anger, he was determined to confront her.

Group of lumberjacks in northern Michigan, 1892. *Library of Congress.*

Unloading lumber near Saginaw, Michigan, 1890. *Library of Congress.*

Before departing, William settled matters of rent with the boarding mistress Mrs. Straight, telling her, "I have a long walk before me." As he began his journey as dusk fell on October 6, crisp autumn leaves crunched under his feet. Initially, he had no intention of returning that night. Hoisting his rifle over his shoulder, he walked deliberately north in the direction of Clarion.

Some hours later, Hattie met him at the front door of her parents' home. William stood on the porch, while she peered back at him from behind the half-open door. They quarreled. Denying him entry to their home, after many bitter words she told him sternly to go away. William left, only to return and wait in the dark outside, holding the rifle he had earlier stashed in the woods.

Patiently, he waited. Through an open window, the kitchen was fully illuminated. When Hattie eventually sat down to supper with her parents, William had a clear view of her profile.

Raising the rifle slowly, he carefully took aim, exhaled and slowly squeezed the trigger. The loud report was soon followed by screams from within.

Shouldering his rifle, William disappeared into the night, returning to Boyne Falls on foot. He did not look back. Being a seasoned hunter, he was fairly certain his shot had been true.

Hunted and Cornered

When Hattie was struck by the bullet, for a brief moment time appeared frozen. Then pandemonium broke out in the Webster home. Hattie slumped over and fell off the chair amid the sudden chaos. Her mother rushed to her side, screaming, and her father assessed the scene, rushing out to notify neighbors.

Charlevoix County Sheriff Henry C. Cooper was sent for, and it did not take long for him to hear about the earlier visit from William Shain. Quickly learning of Shain's residence south in Boyne Falls, Sheriff Cooper assembled a posse, began searching the nearby woods and telephoned the village marshal in Boyne Falls. He ordered the marshal to surround Shain's home and await his arrival on the eleven o'clock evening train.

Men loading a lumber train in northern Michigan, 1892. *Library of Congress.*

William lived on the second floor of the Brookdale house. His room had an entrance by means of an exterior staircase. William made it home before the village marshal had time to take action. When Sheriff Cooper arrived from the train depot, members of the posse called up to William numerous times from below. They implored him to come down the stairs peacefully without his gun, but he refused.

The officers soon enlisted the help of two of Williams's friends to venture up the stairs with them cautiously. As the group slowly ascended, they called out his name, hearing no answer in reply. When they arrived at the second-story landing, one friend spoke through the door, telling William he wanted to enter alone, to return something he borrowed. When William unlocked the door, the friend entered and Sheriff Cooper followed close behind him. It was just before midnight.

Double Tragedy

Inside, William was standing before the bed when the men entered. On seeing the sheriff, he looked at them for a fleeting moment and threw himself backward on the mattress. Simultaneously, he raised a .32-caliber British bulldog revolver to his head and pulled the trigger. The gunshot in the confines of the small room was deafening. The bullet entered his temple, leaving gunpowder burns on his hairline.

All who witnessed this stood in stunned horror near the doorway, immediately assuming he was dead, as blood sprayed up the wall behind the headboard. Nevertheless, William did not die immediately. A doctor was sent for and arrived in short order. He examined the head wound, but there would be no recovery. William lived for about an hour in incoherent misery before finally expiring.

When Hattie had been shot by William, the bullet struck her in the skull. She was killed instantly. William had fled without knowing the outcome, only seeing Hattie collapse from her chair through the open window.

A detailed search of his room later revealed three letters he had written to his sisters and family describing his mad infatuation with Hattie, later deemed the impetus of the crime. Within these letters, he fervently wrote that he hoped he had killed the woman he loved so they would be united in death.

One newspaper described the incident as a "double tragedy that ended an unholy love."

Lumber camp in northern Michigan, 1870. *Library of Congress.*

Logging a big load in Michigan, 1880. *Library of Congress.*

BOYNE FALLS COMPENDIUM

The population of Boyne Falls doubled in the 1890s from 450 to 900 by the 1900 census, driven by the growth of the logging industry, as did Clarion and Boyne City. However, by the mid-1900s, the logging industry had begun to diminish, and around the same time, the railroad became less important, being replaced by the automobile. The population of the small villages went into decline as families moved away.

Today, Boyne Falls is still home to about 350 and is perhaps known best for its ski resorts and tourism.

Sheriff Henry C. Cooper went on the serve as the county treasurer and was later appointed by Governor Albert E. Sleeper in 1918 to serve on the State Board of Corrections and Charities. He passed away at the age of sixty-seven in 1924.

11

A MYSTERIOUS DREAM AND A MISSING BOY

(1898)

One of the most mysterious cases of disappearance ever known in the vicinity occurred last Sunday, and is still under the shadow of doubt.
—The Sunday Record, *October 16, 1898*

On Sunday morning, October 9, 1898, fourteen-year-old Richard Miller Jr. and his father, R.J. Miller Sr., went to the fields on their ten-acre farm off Coldwater Road (present-day Riverside Drive) just south of the millpond (north of Mineral Avenue today) in Battle Creek, Michigan. The two had gone out to feed their cattle and, on their return trip to the house, picked some walnuts and carried them home. Following this, young Richard sat with his mother, Ellen, in the kitchen cracking the nuts for a short time.

Missing

After he had completed his morning chores, Richard did not stay long at home. It was a cool morning in Michigan, and he had plans.

First, he went outside to a neighboring apple tree and picked some fruit. Then he proceeded up the road carrying a cane, which was really just a small section of an old broom handle, eating an apple in the other. He was going to meet some friends about a quarter mile down the road. His friends

An 1873 Atlas showing the Miller farm. *Willard Library Archive.*

were out hunting for hickory nuts, and when they were done, they had made plans the previous day to meet up at the sandbank that morning.

The sandbank was a small hill along Coldwater Road that had eroded and turned into a mix of silica and volcanic rock over time. It was a place where local farmers frequently carved out wagon loads of sand used for tilling into the muddy soil. The sand was also used as a building material for cement and stone foundations. To the children in the community, it was a fun place to play.

That morning in early autumn, the skies were mostly clear. Richard was a medium-sized boy, standing about five feet, five inches tall, weighing about 115 pounds. He had light brown hair and was wearing blue overalls, a light-colored shirt, a gray vest and a narrow-brimmed brown hat that morning. He was seen by several passing neighbors walking down the road knocking apples off a few trees with the stick he carried and later sitting on a pile of sand at the pit, barefooted, eating an apple. Following this, a gap in conflicting witness accounts is where the mystery truly begins.

Richard, for lack of a better description, vanished. The first person to notice was his mother, when he did not return home for lunch that day. His parents were not concerned. They assumed he was just out playing and lost track of time. By late afternoon, however, his parents had become worried and contacted neighbors. Soon an emergency search party had formed, and they went looking.

When they arrived at the sandbank, the searchers found a half-eaten apple, another full apple and his stick, but no sign of Richard. The sandbank hill was where he had last been seen. No one reported seeing the boy walking down the road, and initially there were no reports about whether his friends had ever arrived to meet him.

THE SEARCH BEGINS

The sheriff was soon contacted, and an official search began. Fearing the boy had been buried in a cave-in at the sandbank, although the soil showed no visible evidence of a fresh collapse, neighbors began digging. They dug all over the hillside for several hours. Finally, they exhausted their efforts but had found no sign of him.

The family had relatives in Sonoma, a few miles down the road in the direction of East Leroy, and the idea was presented that perhaps Richard had gone there. Almost immediately after it was suggested, the idea was dismissed. The family knew Richard always came home first whenever he decided to go to Sonoma. He would have wanted to clean up after playing, and this time he had not. Hearing the suggestion, his older brother, however, made the journey to that farm anyway and soon learned he was not there.

Richard had simply disappeared.

Fears quickly grew for his safety. He was not one to run away and did not like to be away from home at night. It was getting dark on the first day of his disappearance, and his parents had become quite concerned.

The next day, a larger search party was formed, and the nearby woods and underbrush surrounding where he was last seen were thoroughly searched. The theory that he was buried in a collapse of the sandbank was again explored, and more digging was done, to no avail.

The nearby millpond and river, just up the road toward town, were considered. The chief of police, town constable and chief of the fire department procured a boat and proceeded up the river looking for signs of the boy. By the end of the second day, there was still no sign of Richard.

On the third and fourth days, the river was searched again, as well as the banks of nearby Graham Lake and Goguac Lake, to no success. Richard's disappearance was becoming a deep mystery for the community. His parents were growing terribly concerned as the days wore on. The weather was getting cooler, and Richard had left without a coat, wearing only a vest.

Rumors and Dead Ends

In the weeks that followed, there were many rumors that surfaced in Battle Creek about the disappearance of Richard Miller. Newly appointed Chief of Police William Farrington had sent a description of the missing boy to other communities, including Albion, Athens, Union City, Sturgis, Climax, Coldwater, Homer, Hillsdale, Vicksburg, Kalamazoo, Jackson, Jonesville, Leonidas, Burr Oak and Lansing.

Farrington even sent word to police chiefs in Evansville and LaGrange, Indiana, in search of a hypnotist named Santanelli who had previously visited Battle Creek. Neighbors theorized that he had hypnotized Richard into going away with him because the boy had enjoyed his performance when he visited the city. The chief of police in Evansville reported that the hypnotist was there, but it became clear after thorough questioning that he had no knowledge of the boy's disappearance.

R.J. Miller, Richard's father, however, was not convinced of Santanelli's innocence. He hired a Grand Rapids detective to assist him in locating the mesmerist. The detective learned that the next show the performer would be at was in Winchester, Kentucky, near the end of October. R.J. personally traveled to Kentucky to confront Santanelli and hunted for the boy all around that town, including visiting the place the performer was staying. He discovered that the companions Santanelli was traveling with were three men, all older than his son. Only then was he satisfied that the showman had nothing to do with his son's disappearance and returned home.

Upon his return, R.J. Miller became convinced his son must be dead. Although he had a wallpaper store in Battle Creek and a small farm, R.J. was not a wealthy man. On November 3, he placed an advertisement in the Battle Creek Moon offering a reward of $25 for the recovery of his son's remains, which was the most cash he could offer at that time. Another friend and downtown merchant who owned a farm implement business, Benjamin Pinch, offered to pay an additional sum of $25. In the weeks and months that followed, R.J. was able to increase the reward to $60, and other neighbors also pitched in, along with an additional $50 being offered from the sheriff department.

On November 9, a month after Richard had gone missing, Chris Martinussen was fishing near the millpond when he pulled up on his line to see a small piece of blue overalls attached to his hook. He tugged at the snag for some time, but eventually his hook gave way and the cloth disappeared back into the water. He reported the incident to the police, informing them the piece of cloth was about one foot in length.

This report sparked a new search of the millrace for Richard. This time, the police and fire department combined forces to drag the bottom near the headgates where the blue cloth had been seen. A large crowd of spectators congregated on the shore watching the search. Discussion was made about draining the millpond for a more thorough investigation if evidence was found, but once again there was no sign of the boy. After a thorough search, the effort was discontinued.

On November 25, a traveling salesman reported seeing a boy who met Richard's description over at a hotel in Hillsdale, and he overheard he was using the name Arthur Miller. Aware of the story of a missing boy named Miller, he notified two local deputies from the sheriff's office, who brought the young man in for questioning. They reportedly asked him if his father's name was R.J. Miller, and he stated it was. They asked him why he was leaving home, and boy told him that he had trouble with his father and left.

After questioning the young man, they released him. When the two deputies were questioned about why they did not bring him to Battle Creek, they responded that their sheriff instructed them to release him. They did, however, confirm that he boarded a train for Eaton Rapids and notified Sheriff Farrington in Battle Creek.

Chief Farrington contacted the Eaton Rapids Sheriff Department, and eventually they apprehended the boy in question. What they discovered was the boy's father was Henry J. Miller, not R.J. Miller, and he had run away from his home because of abuse.

Further proof was that his mother had given him a letter approving of his roaming the region to find work and also eight dollars for use in an emergency. He had previously passed through Battle Creek and was familiar with some of the local business names. He had given this information to the police in Hillsdale. It was a misunderstanding due to the similarity of his father's name with R.J. Miller and Arthur being the same age. The young man was again released, as he was clearly not Richard Miller.

The Dream

As November moved into December, winter weather intensified in Michigan, and all searches for Richard Miller were discontinued until spring. It was during this cold winter weather that an older woman in Union City, Julia Willard, began having dreams about young Richard.

Over and over again she saw in her dreams his body being placed in a wooden box, carried away by a man with a horse and wagon and buried in a marsh near Athens. She would awake each time with the certainty that the boy was dead and she needed to find him. However, it was bitter cold, and she resolved the only thing she could do was wait until spring.

In March 1899, R.J. Miller notified the *Battle Creek Daily Journal* that he would institute a new search for his son along the Kalamazoo River as soon as the frost was out of the ground, and he was looking for volunteers to assist.

By early May, the reward, with total community support, had increased to a sum of $200 from all contributors for the finding or the recovery of the remains of Richard. A newly elected Calhoun County sheriff, Herbert R. Williams, was spearheading a new search effort as well. Hope was renewed that the boy would soon be located safely or his remains located.

On Monday, May 8, Julia Willard, along with her half-sister Matilda Burger, found themselves in Battle Creek through a fortunate train of circumstances, walking on Coldwater Road. Needing a rest on their journey, they stopped at the Miller house for a visit.

When they were ready to resume their walk, Charles Clapp, who was finishing some work for the Millers, offered to take them the rest of the way in his buggy. However, he was eating his lunch and asked if they could wait. They accepted his offer, telling him they would begin walking, and asked him to come along when ready.

The two ladies continued their journey down the road, which took them past the sandbank and beyond that, the farm owned by Frank Holden. When they approached, Julia looked over at Holden's house and barn, and she saw a wagon. The familiarity of the wagon reminded her again of her winter dreams. She paused for a moment, reviewing the memory of her dream while staring as Matilda walked on ahead.

Frank Holden eventually came out of the dwelling, asking her what she was doing standing in front of his house.

"I was just remembering something," Julia replied.

"Well get off my property" was the curt response from Holden, somewhat menacing. Julia resumed her walk down the road toward Matilda and, after a few moments, stopped.

She decided to retrace her steps back past the Holden house for one more look and then continued to the sandbank where Richard had last been seen.

Compelled by the memories of her vision, she decided to dig around in the embankment with a stick. Matilda had followed her, and stood by, familiar with the sometimes-peculiar habits of her sister.

After digging only for a short time, Julia observed a small black object protruding from the hole she had created in the embankment. She later described it as looking like a 'beef's tongue' sticking out of the sand.

She reached over and gave the object a jerk. To her astonishment, she found herself holding onto a blackened human foot. Undaunted, she dug away more of the sand to be sure of what she was seeing.

It was indeed a foot, and it was bare legged up to rolled-up blue pant legs. It was then she knew it matched the description of the missing boy.

Leaving her find without further disturbance, she reported her discovery to the police immediately. After the sheriff arrived, a coroner's inquest was soon organized. The body was excavated and later positively identified as being that of Richard Miller.

Julia told investigators of the dreams and the events of the day that compelled her to visit the sandbank and dig. She also told them that Frank Holden looked like the man she had seen in her dream.

Coroner's Inquest

From the beginning, the police suspected foul play. The investigators' initial assessment was that the body was lying on its side, parallel to the breadth of the sandbank. They believed that if the sand had fallen on him unexpectedly, his body would have been forced with either the head or feet pointing downward. Instead, the boy lay on his side, with his knees almost to his chest.

The postmortem examination was held at undertaker Walter S. Keet's office. The state of decay limited what they could identify, but there was no clear evidence of any marks of violence on him. However, with the state of decomposition, the examining doctors indicated that he might easily have been choked to death without any signs being visible.

Julia was questioned extensively about how she found the body during the investigative hearings of the inquest. Matilda was also questioned in detail and corroborated her story.

Family members who knew Julia scoffed publicly about her "dream" story, but no evidence in the investigation ever revealed that Julia ever had anything to do with or knowledge of the boy's disappearance until it had been reported in the newspapers.

The inquest interviewed over twenty people connected with Richard Miller. One man, Thomas Mitchell, lived on Coldwater Road near the sandbank. When he heard of the disappearance of the Miller boy, he was one of the volunteers who had spent many hours digging at the sandbank looking for the boy.

Thomas told the inquest that he was certain that the body was not there when they searched the entire sandbank on multiple occasions. He testified that the volunteers had dug into the sandbank and tried to excavate a cave to simulate how the boy may have gotten buried, and they could not do it, as the sand always filled in the hole. He maintained it was impossible for the body to have been found where it was without someone placing it there after the initial search.

Charles Hicks also testified that he had dug on three separate days at the sandbank looking for the boy. He reported that where the body was eventually found was covered with dirt at that time, and there was no trace of it having been disturbed. He recalled how they found barefoot prints at the sandy hill in other areas of the embankment, which they presumed were made by Richard, but none were found on the north end where his body was discovered. He was also convinced the body had been placed there after the search.

Eugene Rice, another searcher who used a large earth scraper at the site of the sandbank looking for the boy, maintained that where the body was found, back in October there was over six feet of embankment in front of that area. He, too, was convinced that the body could not have been there when they searched.

R.J. Miller took the stand and recounted the first hours of the search at the sandbank for his son. He remembered seeing the bare footprints, as reported before, and also a man's prints in the area where the body was found. He was also convinced the body of his son was placed where it was found after the search had completed.

Further testimony came from Deputy Sheriff Elliott in which he expressed certainty that where the body was found was intact and undisturbed at the time of the initial search. He was also certain that the body had been placed in the bank after the search ended the prior fall.

Several other volunteers who searched the sandbank also testified that they were convinced that there was no possibility the body was there the multiple times they had searched. One medical doctor testified to having stood by while he had a man slowly sink a long steel rod into the sandbank over and over again when searching for the boy, and they never encountered an obstruction.

Julia's Reward

Having discovered the body, Julia made claim to the offered reward money. R.J. Miller collected all of the funds offered except one. Benjamin Pinch, who had offered twenty-five dollars of the reward, refused to pay.

Pinch did not believe Julia's dream story and suspected she knew more about the boy's death than she was letting on. He was convinced she must have been involved and publicly stated as much.

Julia, in turn, sued Pinch, and he used the opportunity to have his own attorney cross-examine her in court about her knowledge of the boy's disappearance. She did not have any new revelations to share, as Pinch insinuated, and the judge awarded her the twenty-five dollars in his final decision.

Julia Willard had finally received the $200 reward for finding the body. However, her sister Matilda soon demanded half, maintaining that she was present when the discovery was made. Julia initially refused to split it with her.

Matilda then hired an attorney and prepared to sue her sister over the matter, and only then did Julia acquiesce and split the reward with her.

Lyndon Phelps's Story

Speculation lingered in the community that Richard may have been kidnapped, murdered and then placed back in the sandbank after the search for him had ended in late November.

One such person who added kindling to these theories was Lyndon Phelps, a local farmer who was pulling a threshing wheel down Coldwater Road on the morning Richard went missing.

He claimed to have seen an unidentified man pulling a wagon out of the sandbank area as he passed and then heard a sound of what he initially thought was a horse kicking followed by a strange groan.

Phelps had stopped his thresher and turned around, assuming the man had a sick horse and he might need to go over and help him. He looked in the direction of the man, now on the road with the wagon, for a time and heard no other sounds. He decided his services were not needed and so turned back around and continued down the road.

A moment later, he heard what he described as a gruff voice and another low groan, and he stopped and turned around again. The man and the wagon were no longer in sight on the road.

He turned his thresher around and went back up the road. There was no sign of the man or wagon. He described in detail his surroundings, including seeing a barn off the side of the road, which by the time of the inquiry had been torn down.

He believed the sounds of the voices he heard had come from the direction of that barn. He listened for a few minutes and did not hear the sounds again. Puzzled, he made no further investigation and continued his journey down the road as it was getting close to noon, and he had work to get on with.

Later when he learned of the missing Miller boy's body being discovered, he recalled the experience and wondered if what he heard that day was connected. He reported it to the sheriff, who referred him to the coroner's inquest. He testified that the noise he heard could not have come from someone buried under the sand, but that it sounded like it was coming from the wagon that was behind him and later the barn on the side of the road.

Emma Shepard's Story

The evening of the day when Richard went missing, Emma Shepard, who lived on Coldwater Road, across from the Miller farm, was returning in her buggy after going to church in town. She approached a woman and a young girl walking in the road who turned out to be Luella Holden, the wife of Frank Holden, and her twelve-year old daughter, Cora May.

Emma slowed down and greeted Mrs. Holden. She asked her what she heard about the case of the Miller boy across the road, as the Holden farm was adjacent to the sandbank.

In the conversation, Emma learned that Frank Holden had told Luella the circumstances about the boy's disappearance but said he knew nothing more about it. Luella also told Emma that Frank had left that evening on an unexpected errand in a wagon, heading to Athens, and would not be back until morning.

Toward the end of their conversation, Mrs. Holden told Cora May, the young girl standing patiently next to her, to walk home to their house alone, as she needed to continue down the road to see another neighbor before she returned home. Cora May begged her to accompany her to the house first, as she was afraid to walk home alone in the dark, saying, "Something happened lately that frightened me very much."

What that something was the girl would not tell Emma or her mother when they asked. Emma bid Luella goodnight and continued to her farm.

The next day, Emma accompanied Luella to pay a visit to Mrs. Miller and express their sympathy about Richard going missing. After their visit, when they left the Miller home to walk back up the road, Luella confided in Emma that she did not believe the boy was in the sandbank. She thought he was being concealed somewhere else. She elaborated no further on where she came up with this idea.

Emma also testified at the hearing about the barn that Lyndon Phelps mentioned hearing the noises coming from was once located on Frank Holden's farm. She mentioned that Frank Holden had taken his wagon to Athens the same evening after the boy had gone missing. She said the barn was torn down in the days following the boy's disappearance, after Holden returned from Athens. She stated that she never understood why the barn was razed, as it was in the best of condition. She also stated that Frank Holden had then built a new barn, closer to his house.

Could it be that Frank Holden had something to do with Richard Miller's disappearance? Did he encounter the boy sitting at the sandbank, and something happened? Perhaps the boy had said something to him, triggering his temper, followed by a brutal response? Did he then conceal the body and, as in Julia Willard's dream, hide it in Athens and later return and bury it in the sandbank after the search was called off in November?

Frank Holden did have a reputation for having a temper. In addition to his encounter with Julia on the day she discovered the body, in prior years it had been reported in the newspaper that he had been in a fistfight in his own home with another man over the matter of a crying baby, likely when his daughter was very little. In that case, the other man was charged and fined over the incident.

Just a Tragedy?

Later, a twelve-year-old who used to play with Richard at the sandbank testified. The boy revealed that he and Richard had on occasion dug holes in the sandbank to crawl inside, and one time the bank had caved in on Richard. Only Richard's feet were sticking out that time, and he and another companion had pulled him out.

On the morning when Richard was last seen, Agnes Eberstein and her friend Sallie Palmer were driving to Union City along Coldwater Road. When passing the sandbank, Agnes observed a young boy near the top of the embankment. At the time, she thought he was sick, as she was surprised at the strange position he was in.

She revealed that she saw him lying in a large hole in the bank with only his head and shoulders protruding. She thought it was strange that he did not look up when their rig rode past, and she watched him carefully. He was lying on his side and had an apple in his hand. The coroner's inquest had her visit the sandbank and show them exactly where she saw the boy, which was in a different location from where he was found. Sallie Palmer was also interviewed, and she corroborated Agnes's account of events.

Those who believed Richard's death was a tragic accident gained a lot of traction with public sentiment following an August 1899 incident. That is when a nine-year-old girl, Theda Sprague, was playing with some friends at a similar sandbank in the same area, right after several loads of sand had been drawn from the bottom. This created an embankment overhang. Suddenly, while the children were playing, an avalanche of sand came down, completely covering Theda.

Her playmates immediately ran to the home of her mother, quite a distance away, and alerted her. Mrs. Sprague ran to the site but was powerless to do anything at first, as she had taken no tools with her. She notified some men working nearby. They quickly seized shovels, brought them to the sandpit and began digging. Not an article of clothing was visible of Theda beneath the sand. However, they did have the other children to guide them where to dig.

After several minutes of digging, a shovel struck her hand and another her hat, and moments later her limp body was pulled out. She was purple in color and by all appearances deceased.

By good fortune, a physician had arrived during the excavation and was able to clear what little sand was in her airways and resuscitated her. Soon color returned to the little girl's face, and although she had been buried for almost twenty minutes, she was alive.

It was believed the falling sand had forced her hat over her face, keeping her nostrils and mouth mostly clear, which probably saved her life. What was noted by the rescuers was that her body was found in the same position as Richard Miller's had been, and it was clear after that revelation that the boy may have experienced a similar collapse.

Other witnesses later reported to the coroner's inquest seeing other children playing above the sandbank that morning, near a stump that was somewhat of a landmark. Could it be those were his friends who had come to meet and play with him, and they inadvertently caused an avalanche while Richard was napping in a self-made cave he dug below their line of sight?

Mystery and Epitaph

The results of the coroner's inquest were inconclusive. Although there was testimony that asserted Richard's body must have been placed where it was found, there was little proof beyond speculation. It remained possible he was abducted and maybe even murdered in another location and then returned to where he was found. Evidence, however, was lacking to prove this other than the certainty of the searchers who had investigated the sandbank on three separate occasions.

There were also strong witness testimonies that pointed toward it being an accident, as noted earlier.

Either scenario, foul play or tragedy, lacked evidence to prove conclusively. Was his death just a tragic accident? Did the boy dig a hole, take a nap and become hopelessly trapped from a cave-in? Did his friends arrive that morning and not see him below, inadvertently burying him?

Or did something more sinister happen to Richard? What were those sounds that Phelps heard coming from the wagon behind

Richard Miller headstone at Oak Hill Cemetery, Battle Creek, Michigan. *Author collection.*

him and later from the Holden barn? Why did Frank Holden, the neighbor, leave suddenly that night to go to Athens in a wagon and then tear down his perfectly good barn upon his return? What frightened Holden's daughter so that she did not want to walk home at night? Did something happen in Frank Holden's barn?

Then there is the mystery surrounding Julia Willard. Did she really have a vision, or was she somehow involved in the crime? Did she really get lucky in finding the body? Or were the dreams just a story she invented to get attention or perhaps provide a cover story for something else? She testified the man in her dreams looked like Frank Holden. Was this all just a strange coincidence or really some supernatural experience?

Mystery still surrounds the death of Richard Miller Jr. What happened at the sandbank that morning in October 1898 may never be known. The State of Michigan registry on his death reads "Cause of death unknown." His death certificate simply states, "Death caused by violence. How and by what means unknown."

He was buried at Oak Hill Cemetery, and the epitaph on his stone reads:

> *Richard J. Miller, Jr. Lost October 9, 1898. Laid to rest here May 9, 1899. Aged 14 years.*

12

DARK WATERS AND WHISKEY GEORGE

(1899)

Justice is sometimes slow but it was not very snail-like in the case of Boucher.
—The Evening News, *January 1, 1900*

St. Joseph and Benton Harbor, Michigan, are twin port cities on Lake Michigan. The mouth of the St. Joseph River is an inland waterway that has long been used for shipping traffic, although the familiar sight today is mostly recreational boating. As the river makes its way inland, it intersects with the Paw Paw River, which takes a northerly direction into Benton Harbor. After passing the Paw Paw, the St. Joseph River winds southward, forming the northern shoreline of the older city of St. Joseph.

Although only a portion remains today, there once existed a robust shipping canal in Benton Harbor, which officially opened in 1863. The canal began at the St. Joseph River, intersected with the Paw Paw River and delivered a straight waterway for shipping into the enterprising new village at the terminus. The canal passed under a drawbridge before continuing on northward to rejoin the Paw Paw River through a series of smaller canals.

In 1881, the Chicago & West Michigan Railway was formed and built tracks through Benton Harbor. The railway began in La Crosse, Indiana; passed through New Buffalo; and crossed the St. Joseph River, splitting into two tracks that crossed over the Paw Paw River. The eastern branch of the twin tracks followed the banks of the shipping canal with a stop at the Lakeshore Lumber Company before it reunited with the western track north of the village, stopping at the passenger depot. By 1899, the railway line ran through Holland and Grand Rapids and continued all the way to Kalkaska. By the end of that year, the company had consolidated with two other railway companies to form the Pere Marquette Railway.

On the opposite shore of the shipping canal ran a streetcar line that connected St. Joseph and Benton Harbor. Today the railroad is long gone, and the iron bridge over the former eastern branch of the C&WM Railway that once crossed over the Paw Paw River is now a footpath. The path of the old streetcar line that once had a bridge over the St. Joseph River and followed the western bank of the shipping canal has been replaced by the bicentennial bridge on West Main Street. The streetcar lines are a distant memory, but on a summer evening in 1899, men were stationed by the C&WM Railway tending to the drawbridge near the heart of the village.

On Thursday evening, August 17, 1899, Berrien County Sheriff Edgar H. Ferguson was called to the riverbanks by Richard Lysaght, a familiar village resident from his decades serving as the drawbridge tender in Benton Harbor, who now rented boats near that same location. Lysaght reported the discovery of a human body floating face down where the canal joined the Paw Paw River north of the village. The body appeared to have floated down the canal before it drifted into some rocks near the mouth of the river.

When extracted from the water, the bloated corpse was determined to be of a man with a large contusion on his face. The former bridge tender, who was on hand during the removal of the corpse from the river, informed the

Map of Benton Harbor showing the canal, 1889. *Library of Congress.*

sheriff that he had seen that man being led across the bridge the previous evening in the company of another man who was familiar to him. He did not know the identity of the older man found in the river. Lysaght and his co-worker George Brown both recalled seeing them walk past on the bridge the evening before while they were working on their boats.

The man leading the older man was carrying a satchel over his shoulder and a big stick. When they were about fifteen feet away, Lysaght spoke to the older man, who did not respond and simply continued to walk forward across the bridge. The men passed into the night toward the village.

Unidentified Body

A short while later, Lysaght and Brown heard what Lysaght described as unearthly yells coming from the direction the two men had gone. After listening in the dark for a time and not hearing anything further, they had dismissed the noises as being the sounds of someone falling down, perhaps a stumbling drunk leaving from a nearby tavern.

The following evening, Lysaght was notified by William Fuller, who worked for the Bradford Paper Company, that he had spotted a body floating near the headwaters of the Paw Paw River. Soon after, Lysaght contacted the sheriff.

Sheriff Ferguson initially concluded in his preliminary examination that the man had likely fallen and hit his head on a rock and drowned. Perhaps he had been drinking and stumbled while navigating the rocks along the embankment of the canal or river or had just fallen in the dark hitting his head on some hard surface.

Later that evening, the body of the unidentified man was taken to Jasper Rowe's Undertaking Room located just up the hill on High Street. Jasper Rowe was known as "Jap" to his friends, and his family were long-standing and well-known grocers in the village. Jasper had been the first in the family to break into a new line of business as an undertaker.

That same night, a local man, George Boucher, otherwise known around town as "Whiskey George" because of his frequency at the taverns, had stopped by Rowe's Undertaking Room to view the body in the company of a few other men.

A former sheriff, Charles Henry Whitcomb, who now resided in nearby St. Joseph, also made an appearance at the undertaker's that evening. He

Water Street in Benton Harbor, circa 1895. *Clark Engraving & PTG Co. Milwaukee.*

had heard about the discovery and came to see if he could assist with the identification.

While viewing the body, Boucher shivered noticeably when he looked at the deceased. Whitcomb, who observed him, asked, "Did you ever see this man before?" Boucher replied, "I have… I saw him sitting on the back steps of Fonger's Saloon." He informed Whitcomb that he was in the alley behind the Hotel Benton when he saw him. That was the extent of the conversation.

It so happened that Richard Lysaght arrived at the undertaker's office right about this time and immediately recognized Boucher as having been the one he had seen in the company of the deceased man earlier in the evening. He overheard the brief exchange between Boucher and Whitcomb, and notified Sheriff Ferguson the next day.

On receiving the report, Sheriff Ferguson immediately went in search of George Boucher around the village, only to discover he had disappeared. It did not take long for the sheriff to become increasingly suspicious of the potential suspect when he learned from storeowners in town that Whiskey George had been seen about the village on Wednesday freely spending money on a new suit and boarding a train for Chicago Thursday evening after his encounter at the undertaker's.

By the time the sheriff had made this connection, the body of the still unidentified man had already been buried in Crystal Springs Cemetery. He quickly notified Justice of the Peace John St. Clair, who also served as the county coroner. St. Clair ordered the body exhumed and then empaneled a six-member coroner's jury to investigate and review the facts of the case in a formal hearing.

He instructed Dr. Wakeman Ryno to conduct a thorough postmortem examination of the deceased. Accompanying Dr. Ryno was Dr. Henry V. Tutton. The two doctors soon concluded in their examination that the man had been a victim of assault and not an accidental injury.

It was Monday morning when Sheriff Ferguson boarded a train to Chicago in search of Whiskey George.

Chicago Arrest

George Boucher did not prove difficult to locate in the Windy City. Sheriff Ferguson enlisted the help of Chicago city detectives, and they soon found Boucher sitting on a box, not far from a warehouse outside of a saloon on the Graham & Morgan docks, and arrested him. When the sheriff approached Boucher, he said, "Hello, George," and Boucher jumped to his feet, startled and surprised to see him.

Ferguson told him he was wanted and produced a warrant. Boucher, somewhat under the influence, at once began to protest his innocence. Initially, he was taken to the Central Police Station in Chicago and was cool and collected. However, after he was placed in a cell, Boucher, who was generally regarded as a tough character, broke down in despair.

By Tuesday, news had returned to Benton Harbor that Sheriff Edgar Ferguson arrested Whiskey George in Chicago. George was sobering up when he returned with the sheriff to the Berrien County jail in St. Joseph. On Wednesday, he was taken before Justice St. Clair and arraigned.

Boucher entered a plea of not guilty and, having no further evidence to present, was bound over to the Circuit Court under bonds of $1,800. Being unable to furnish the money for his own release, he was ordered to await trial in the county jail. The judge ordered a hearing set for the following Friday, September 1.

While in jail, Boucher was overtaken with a bout of delirium tremens. He lay on his cot sweating, shaking and howling as the effects of alcohol withdrawal at its extreme took its toll. He refused to eat and begged the deputies to bring him some alcohol, which he was denied.

Due to his condition, the sheriff and the court determined that he would not be able to testify on the events of the prior Thursday evening for several days. Boucher instead lay in his cell, occasionally being given cold compresses and water and eating very little food, waiting for his condition to improve.

By the Friday of the scheduled hearing, he was finally on the downward trend of the withdrawal, although he was described as being in a general nervous state. The formal inquest was able to resume in the courts, and the proceedings began.

Attorney Frank P. Graves, from the newly formed law firm Graves & Wilson, was appointed to represent Boucher, and he was confident they would have no trouble in obtaining an acquittal for him. The prosecuting attorney was George Milton Valentine, who at the time had practiced law for over twenty years and had just been elected to his second term as Berrien County prosecutor. Valentine worked closely with the sheriff's department to collect and submit evidence.

Inquest

The official inquest was a preliminary hearing to review the facts and determine whether the local justice would recommend the case going to trial. Justice of the Peace John St. Clair presided over the hearing.

Dr. Ryno and Dr. Tutton both testified at the hearing about their examination of the body, clarifying that they autopsied only the right lung. Their inspection found it was filled with air in the upper lobe, and the lower lobe was solid. They indicated a drowned person's lung is often bloody and frothy with mucous, and in this case, that condition was absent. Therefore, it was impossible to swear that the man had conclusively died of drowning. Not only was there an absence of mucous in the lung, but there was also no indication of water found in the throat.

There was a deep laceration on the man's face, but Dr. Ryno, when questioned about this on the witness stand, indicated it would be difficult to determine whether this wound was received before or after the man struck the water. He admitted the injury may have come from falling on a stone, but in either case, he believed that the blow came before death.

The conclusion in their investigation was that he had been struck on the head and that injury was likely the cause of his death before he fell into or was placed in the river.

When Boucher was arrested by Sheriff Ferguson in Chicago, the shirt he wore was blood splattered, and there was a larger stain of blood on the shoulder. The sheriff had bought Boucher a new shirt and retained the original shirt as evidence, submitting it at the inquest to be examined by the jury.

Jasper Rowe, the undertaker, was called to the witness stand to verify the exhibits presented that were found on the deceased. The inventory included underwear, hat, handkerchief, vest, pants and coat. He indicated he believed the items were the same clothing articles found on the man when he was brought to his office. Other witnesses confirmed that no money was found on the dead man.

While in custody, Boucher denied any involvement. When Richard Lysaght testified to seeing him on the bridge that evening, Boucher did not deny it. He explained he had gone fishing with the stranger, and they had parted ways after crossing the bridge. He maintained he was genuinely surprised at the undertaker's to learn his fishing companion was the body they found.

The inquest into the death of the unknown man resulted in a recommendation by the jury to the presiding judge to charge George Boucher with murder.

The official conclusion of the six-panel jury was submitted:

> *The body when found bore marks of violence in that it appeared that the deceased had been struck a heavy blow with some blunt instrument or club across the right cheek bone, cutting the flesh and breaking the nose over. There were also marks of violence upon face of said deceased person and so the jurors, upon their oaths say, that death must have occurred before the body of said deceased entered the water, and we do further believe said deceased came to his death by unlawful means and that we have reasonable grounds to believe and do believe that one George Boucher is guilty of striking the blow that caused the death of the said deceased, either as a principal or accessory, and we do recommend that the said George Boucher be held for trial.*

The Trial of George Boucher

The trial was scheduled for September and arranged to be presided over by Judge Orville W. Coolidge of the Second Circuit Court.

During the trial, Richard Lysaght was questioned about encountering Boucher on the bridge that evening with the victim. He explained that he had called out to the old man when he saw him in the company of Boucher and cautioned him to be careful with his money.

The prosecuting attorney asked him why he had told the man to be careful, and Lysaght replied, "I knew Boucher pretty well and knew his character was pretty shady."

At this answer, Boucher, sitting at the defense table, threw back his head and laughed loudly in the courtroom.

Again the medical doctors were brought in to testify, once again confirming their belief that the cause of death was the blow to the head and not drowning.

The defense attorney, Graves, argued that given the body was found near where the canal joined the Paw Paw River, the murder must have happened in that location, which did not align with the witness statements placing Boucher on the drawbridge over the ship canal near the village. Graves emphasized his client had gone fishing with the stranger, and as stated during the inquest, they had parted ways after crossing the bridge. Boucher left the man unharmed.

Prosecutor Valentine argued that man could have been killed near the bridge and then thrown into the canal. Over a twenty-four-hour period, the body could have been moved in the currents of shipping vessels in the direction of where it was found near the river. He pointed out there were no witnesses who saw Boucher and the man fishing, nor did anyone see them part ways after the sighting on the bridge.

To that point in the trial, all of the evidence presented by Valentine, including the witness testimony, although compelling, was circumstantial. The bloody shirt could be tested as to whether it was human blood, but there existed no other method to prove it came from the victim. Sheriff Ferguson, however, had a few more surprise witnesses for the prosecution.

Jailhouse Informants

Two jailhouse informants were brought forward. One was Lee Taylor, a Black man from Niles, who was eventually found guilty of burglary and sent to the Ionia penitentiary for fifteen months. The other man was Charles Huss, also from Niles, who was serving fifty days in the county jail for larceny, having been caught stealing a gold watch and chain from a woman. Taylor and Huss claimed George Boucher had conversations with them while they shared a neighboring cell in the Berrien County jail.

Lee Taylor was a frequent visitor to the county jail. This time, he was arrested for an altercation in Niles. Taylor had been at a billiard hall owned by Martin Snodgrass, another Black man. He played a game, and going against the pool hall rules, he had refused to pay. Snodgrass demanded payment, and Taylor pulled out a knife. Countering this, Snodgrass pulled out a revolver and pulled the trigger. The first cartridge failed to explode, and once more in quick succession, he pulled the trigger again.

This time, the .38-caliber round went tearing through Taylor's arm. The victim ran out of the building, traveling about one block, before he realized he had been shot. He looked down, and blood was oozing out of his clothing. The police soon arrived, and Taylor was taken to the hospital. The wound was probed, and the bullet, which had passed near his collarbone, was removed. Both Taylor and Snodgrass were arrested, and more information came out in the investigation that Taylor had burglarized another man's home before arriving at the billiard hall that evening.

Charles Huss was arrested following a complaint by a woman named Mary Summers, whom he had accompanied to a park one evening. They claimed that a man who was impersonating a police officer accosted them in the park, and while the man detained Summers, Huss had run off. During the time he was gone, Summers noticed her gold watch and chain had gone missing. Huff returned only when the other man had left, which was considered a strange report to the real police who investigated.

Mary Summers, however, maintained it was true and gave a description of another man in town named Harry Swartz as the false police officer; he was brought in for questioning. But Swartz was able to prove through an alibi that he was nowhere near the park where the incident happened.

Rather than give up on the case, the police began to investigate Huss. They eventually caught him in the act of trying to pawn the gold watch and chain that Summers had reported missing, and he was arrested and charged with larceny. That was how both Taylor and Huss came to be in the jail at the same time as Boucher.

Both Taylor and Huss testified that Boucher admitted to killing the old man but told them it was unintentional, as he never meant to hit him so hard when he struck the blow to the head. To cover up the crime, he had thrown the victim into the canal. They claimed Boucher's motive for killing the man was robbery. Allegedly, he found only $18.30 in the man's pockets after striking him.

Identity Found

Up until the formal inquest, the identity of the man found in the river had eluded investigators. The man was described as five feet, five inches tall, 150 pounds and wearing dark clothes, a negligee shirt, a black soft hat and lace shoes. The underwear bore a laundry mark of "M.S.G." He had a full beard, very long and gray, and his hair was sandy brown. He had the appearance of being a laboring man of Irish descent. A photo was taken of the man at the funeral home, circulated in the community and even published in the newspapers. At first, no one recognized him.

In early September, two members of the local U.S. Life-Saving Service crew believed they recognized the depiction of the man. The newspapers soon carried the story that the body was of a man named Smith who lived alone in Benton Harbor and was in the habit of fishing near the north pier. Smith was rumored to always carry a large roll of bills on his person, and robbery was the theory behind the murder. This story evaporated a few days later when Smith was found alive and well.

It was only during the trial in early October that the correct identity of the man was found. His name proved to William Hawkins, from Michigan City, Indiana. An attorney named William Breise in Michigan City had received a photo from Prosecutor Valentine, who was a former law partner. It had been reported in Indiana newspapers on September 11 that William Hawkins, described at seventy years of age, had mysteriously disappeared.

Breise showed the photo to Hawkin's daughter, Elizabeth McAdams, who confirmed his identity. Hawkins had lived with Elizabeth and left home on August 15 without telling her where he was going.

Hawkins served the Union in the Civil War with the Twenty-Ninth Indiana Infantry Regiment, which had organized at La Porte, Indiana, in August 1861. His regiment saw engagements at the Battles of Shiloh, Stones River and Chickamauga and many others before he mustered out in December 1865.

The day after he left, Hawkins mailed a letter to Elizabeth from St. Joseph. In that letter, he apologized for his sudden disappearance, saying he disliked saying goodbye. His reasons for leaving and traveling to St. Joseph or Benton Harbor were not stated. After she received the one letter, there had been no further communication from her father.

One mystery that was never solved was the whereabouts of Hawkins's trunk, which had disappeared from his home when he left. How this was disposed of remained unknown to authorities. An additional mystery was why he had made the trip to Michigan, and for what purpose. Was he looking for work? Meeting someone? Or was there another reason he wanted to leave the home of his daughter where he had lived the past few years and start over?

His wife had passed away two years before when he lived in the South Bend area, and he moved in with his daughter. Was he feeling he was a burden to his daughter? Was he still grieving over the loss of his wife, and his daughter was a constant reminder of that? Elizabeth and friends who knew him never received a clear reason for his departure.

Shipping canal in Benton Harbor, circa 1890. *V.O. Hammon Pub. Co. Chicago.*

Convicted

On Friday, November 3, the courtroom was packed with spectators as the attorneys made their final arguments. Frank P. Graves argued that the evidence against his client, Boucher, was entirely circumstantial. He pressed the argument that the body was discovered nowhere near where his client had been seen on the evening before and that the testimony from fellow convicts could hardly be considered reliable. He argued his client had maintained his innocence from the time he was arrested and claimed he never spoke with Taylor or Huss.

Prosecutor Valentine pressed the issues of the body having plenty of time to drift to where it was found, that Boucher was seen in the company of the man the evening before and that the testimony from Taylor and Huss was valid, as they had come forward with their statements on their own. He also pressed on the evidence of the bloody shirt, along with the eyewitness statements, presenting the image of a drunk Boucher who murdered Hawkins with intent to rob him.

The jury in the trial of George Boucher went into deliberations around eight o'clock at night. The crowd remained buzzing with speculation and interest in what the outcome would be. A little over an hour later, just after nine o'clock, they returned with a verdict of guilty of murder in the first degree.

When the verdict was read, Boucher made very little comment. He exhibited a nervous manner throughout the trial and did the same as he awaited the verdict. He did not break down or appear disheartened when the foreman of the jury read their decision to Judge Coolidge. He was overheard making a comment to Sheriff Ferguson that the jurors were "all liars," and added, "Well, I suppose they are all satisfied now," as he was led back to the jail for the weekend.

On Monday afternoon, November 6, Judge Coolidge sentenced George Boucher to hard labor for life at the Michigan State Penitentiary in Jackson. Coolidge asked the condemned man if he had anything to say, and Boucher replied that he was innocent before God and man, asserting the jury did not weigh the evidence. He also stated that he had never spoken with Taylor and Huss, denying their claims.

Boucher was taken by train to prison on Tuesday, November 7, 1899.

Appeals to the Board of Pardons

In December 1901, a little over two years after Boucher had been sent to prison, through his attorneys, he managed to appeal his case for review to the Michigan Board of Pardons. The premise of his request was that the entire case against him was circumstantial.

The Board of Pardons did not officially meet to review his case until April 29, 1902. Instead of meeting in Lansing, they held their meeting at the Hotel Whitcomb in St. Joseph, Michigan. The location was selected so that they could review the chain of evidence against Boucher for the murder of William Hawkins. The board spent two days reviewing the material but decided to take no action in Boucher's case, and he remained in prison.

Despite this development, George Boucher maintained his innocence. In 1911, after serving twelve years as a model prisoner, Boucher still reiterated his innocence to the guards.

In October of that year, Fred Alden, a patrolman from St. Joseph, escorted another prisoner to the Jackson prison and asked to see Boucher. When Boucher came out, he did not recognize the patrolman.

Alden said, "You don't know me, do you, George?"

George replied, "No, I don't. But I am glad to know someone asked for me, for I am serving for a crime I never committed. I am as innocent as you are."

The patrolman then asked if he remembered who used to be in the life-saving service in St. Joseph. After a moment, George's eyes brightened with recognition. "You are not Fred Alden, are you?"

"The same fellow," replied the patrolman. With that, George grasped both of the Alden's hands with vigor, showing appreciation with the gesture of St. Joseph friendship. Alden then told him there were several residents of the area of both St. Joseph and Benton Harbor who believed he never committed the crime he was incarcerated for.

Newspapers back in Berrien County reported on the story and began stoking the efforts to bring clemency to Boucher through the pardon board and Governor Chase Osborn's office. A petition was circulated throughout Berrien County and submitted to the State Board of Pardons in early 1913. Despite this community effort, no further action was taken by the board, and the story faded away again. That would change all too soon.

Drunken Confession

In January 1914, a former convict from Muskegon who had been sentenced to the State Reformatory at Ionia for two years for gross indecency, Horace "Butch" Congdon, broke his parole and went on the run.

He was eventually arrested in Mattoon, Illinois, in March after evading police for two months. Congdon had been in town for about three weeks selling harness oil and spending the money in saloons each night. He had made the mistake of boasting while drunk about having broken his parole in Ionia, telling bartenders, "They are after me, but they will never get Butch Congdon down here!" Someone eventually tipped off the police, and he was picked up and taken to the station.

Shortly after he was arrested in Mattoon, he was placed in a cell. Congdon began pacing up and down, wringing his hands in a highly nervous state. He asked an officer on duty, "Will you call a Catholic priest?"

The officer responded, "What do you want a Catholic priest for?"

"I want to make a confession," replied Congdon.

"Are you Catholic?"

"No," said Congdon, "but I have something on my mind I want to tell."

It happened that the Catholic priest in the area was out of the city at the time, so the police asked if he wouldn't mind just making the confession to them.

"I suppose so," said Congdon.

He then stated the following: "I just wanted to say that I murdered a man in St. Joe, Michigan, fifteen years ago. I hit him in the head with a club and threw his body into the canal. I never saw the poor fellow after that. I wanted to tell this years ago, but I never had the nerve. Oh, poor George Boucher, poor George Boucher."

In St. Joseph, Michigan, the police chief was now former patrolman Fred Alden. Mattoon Police Chief Henry Raymond Scheef notified his office, reporting the confession, misunderstanding the content of what Congdon was saying, believing the murder victim was George Boucher.

The telegram read: "Have Horace Congdon. Has confessed to killing George Boucher; threw body in canal. Congdon violated parole in Ionia. H.R. Scheef, Chief of Police."

Despite this, Chief Alden understood the message and in turn relayed the information to the warden at the Jackson prison.

Warden Simpson at the Michigan State Penitentiary had George Boucher collected from his cell. The guard found the inmate in bed asleep and brought him to the front office. He told Boucher of the confession of Horace Congdon.

Boucher, now sixty years old with a prison pallor, had a stooped back from years of working in the prison box factory. When the news was told to him, at first he was unable to grasp the meaning, and after a few minutes became composed and touched his cheeks while looking at the officers, responding, "O God, if it's only true. Do you think it is? Will Congdon stick to his story? Will he free me after all of these years I have suffered, an innocent man?"

During the time Boucher had been incarcerated, his father, mother, brother and two sisters had all died. He had only one remaining sister still living in Detroit.

Boucher wept in front of the warden saying, "Thank God Almighty that I am to be free!"

The warden notified the Board of Pardons of the developments, and they responded on March 31 that the case would have to go before newly elected Governor Woodbridge Ferris, as Boucher was a lifer. The petition submitted by the Berrien County residents was still pending.

Meanwhile, Chief Alden left the following day for Mattoon to learn the details of the confession firsthand while Congdon was in custody. Chief Alden interviewed Congdon in his cell, and when confronted with the questions, he repudiated his murder confession. Here is what Chief Alden reported that Congdon said when he confronted him and asked him about his previous story:

> *Oh. I just put one over on the police here. You know I have been drunk for a week and I wanted a little excitement, so I told them that I had murdered a man back in Michigan. They were fools enough to believe me. You know that Butch Congdon is the biggest drunkard in the country and when drunk he is the biggest liar in the country. There's nothing to this. I wasn't in St. Joe when the murder was committed.*

Despite this statement, Chief Alden was not convinced that the notorious character did not kill Hawkins. Even if he was drunk, how and why did he recall a murder that happened fifteen years ago? How did he know so much about the case, including the names and principals and other details about the crime?

According to the Mattoon police, Congdon had stuck to his story until they informed him the St. Joseph police were on the way to question him. He immediately began making the claim that there was nothing to his story, even before Chief Alden arrived. So when Alden arrived, Congdon was vociferous in his denial, and no amount of grilling would move him from his new story.

Chief Alden decided to investigate to see if Congdon had, in fact, been in the St. Joseph and Benton Harbor area during the time of the murder. He began making arrangements to bring Congdon back with him to St. Joseph to be questioned by the former prosecutor, Milton Valentine, and then transferred to the Jackson prison.

Before Alden could complete the arrangements, Warden Fuller of the Ionia State Reformatory sent Keeper I.L. Cotton to collect Congdon and return him. Warden Fuller was doubtful of Congdon's confession, believing the man mentally deficient, though not insane. Chief Alden's plans to question him further evaporated.

Records would show that the forty-four-year-old Congdon was born in New Hudson, Michigan, and as small boy moved to St. Joseph, where he lived twenty years. In discovering this history, Chief Alden determined it was feasible that Congdon was in the St. Joseph and Benton Harbor area at the time of the murder.

When Boucher returned to work in the prison box factory waiting for news from the Board of Pardons, guards and fellow inmates offered him congratulations.

Pardoned

Two more years would pass following the Congdon confession and retraction. Chief Alden, many citizens in Berrien County and even Warden Simpson rallied in support of Boucher's release, pressing the Board of Pardons. Without the confession of Congdon, however, or any new evidence, despite the suspicions of law enforcement, there was slow progress.

Governor Ferris refused to act without a recommendation from the Board of Pardons. In 1916, George Schneider, the president of the Board of Pardons, finally agreed to review the request for pardon by George Boucher.

On March 18, he released a statement indicating that he was going to investigate the home of the sister of Boucher in Detroit, and if the surroundings were determined to be favorable, he would recommend to Governor Ferris to parole him on the grounds of good behavior under the law.

Boucher would ultimately be released later that same year. He moved into the home of his sister.

Finally free, George Boucher would eke out a meager living sharpening scissors and other household instruments and doing some carpentry. On January 26, 1922, he moved back to Berrien County destitute and applied for admittance to the County Poor House. He was admitted to the facility and passed away on February 22, 1922.

BIBLIOGRAPHY

Introduction

Anderson, Janna Quitney. *Imagining the Internet: Personalities, Predictions, Perspectives*. Rowman & Littlefield, 2005.

Delaware, Michael. *Victorian Southwest Michigan True Crime*. The History Press, 2024.

Evening News (Battle Creek, MI). January 1, 1916.

Farhud, Dariush D., and Marjan Zarif Yeganeh. "A Brief History of Human Blood Groups. *Iranian Journal of Public Health* 42, no. 1 (2013): 1–6. https://pmc.ncbi.nlm.nih.gov.

Krasnow, Judy Gail. *Jacktown: History & Hard Times at Michigan's First State Prison*. The History Press, 2017.

Right on Track: A History of the Railroads in Eaton County, Michigan. Eaton County Historical Commission, 2019.

Swisher, Clarice. *Victorian England*. Greenhaven Press, 2000.

Victorian Britain: A Brief History. Historical Association U.K., 2023.

Note

For a complete bibliography on chapters 1–12, visit Michael Delaware.com.

INDEX

N

O

P

R

S

T

U

V

W

ABOUT THE AUTHOR

Michael Delaware is an Arizona native who left home at age eighteen. He lived fifteen years in Georgia, where he worked as a craftsman, artist, salesperson, manager and owner of a stained and decorative glass door and window business. In 1999, he moved to Ann Arbor, Michigan, and from 2001 to the present he has lived in Battle Creek, where he runs his own real estate brokerage firm.

Raised by a hardworking father who was also a storyteller and a mother who was an avid reader and librarian, he has long valued the importance of learning about the past and finding a good story. He has continued his passion for discovering local history in the many places along his life's journey.

He has a YouTube channel under his own name and a popular regional podcast, *Tales of Southwest Michigan's Past*. He is passionate about researching forgotten stories from the Victorian era and is known for his programs on local cemetery, landmark and biographical history.

He volunteers at the Battle Creek Regional History Museum, serving as the marketing director, and when he is not researching and writing, he organizes and promotes multiauthor events around Michigan.

His first true crime collection, *Victorian Southwest Michigan True Crime*, was released in 2024 through The History Press. He is a sought-after public speaker and can be contacted through MichaelDelaware.com.